FROM THE WYE TO THE THAMES.

ley.

CONTENTS.

INTRODUCTION.

The Hereford to Oxford railway line runs through some of the most attractive countryside in England. Whether you like rolling hills, flat plains, riversides or even an exhilarating view from on high, there is something for you, the walker, along this route. Many ramblers like point-to-point walks rather than circular ones, but then there is the problem of how to get back. Complicated car arrangements have to be devised, but, even this is not always a practicable proposition, especially if you only have one car. The Cotswold Line Promotion Group has always tried to encourage the use of trains by ramblers and has, on several occasions, organised properly led rambles. It felt that there was a need for some do-it-yourself rambles, giving fairly precise details of the routes, involving the use of a train. The outcome is this series of station-to-station walks, some of which can be linked together if you are feeling energetic. We chose a west to east direction as this fits in better with the train service, especially at some of the smaller stations. Whilst all the walks involve an element of train travel, you can, if you wish, spend a week or two over them by staying overnight en-route. The choice is yours. "These boots are made for walking", so says the song, so "start walking".

This publication has received the support of Thames Trains Ltd, who operate many of the services on the line.

FOR YOUR GUIDANCE.

The series of walks is arranged numerically from 1 to 12, starting at Hereford and ending at Oxford. In two cases, alternative routes are given and these have an "A" after the number.

There is a short introduction to each walk and this is followed by detailed instructions which should enable most people to complete the route without getting lost. However, the Cotswold Line Promotion Group cannot accept any liability for any inaccuracy in this publication. The walks were researched by volunteer members of the Group and, as far as the Group is aware, were accurate at the time of research (1993-1995). The left hand columns show mileages, the first from the last instruction, the second from the start of the walk. Also shown are the Ordnance Survey grid references. We have also included route maps but, the scale of these, (which varies slightly from map to map, depending on the amount of space available) is too small to give adequate detail. It is recommended that you have with you a large scale map for the area and, for this reason, we have also shown the numbers for the Ordnance Survey 1:50,000 "Landranger" series. Even better of course is the 1.25,000 "Pathfinder" series. Almost all of the route is on public roads or rights of way and much is waymarked (yellow for footpaths and blue for bridleways). The few exceptions are identified as such and are understood to be widely used locally.

You can decide whether to use the train for your outward or return journey. Please obtain a copy of the current rail timetable for the route. These are available from Tourist Information Centres and all staffed stations along the route. It is especially important, if you are relying on a train for your return journey, to allow adequate time for your walk. You can never tell what obstacles you may encounter. A field may be recently ploughed or a pathway overgrown. Similarly, things are continually changing. Stiles can be replaced by gates - we found no less than six of these in the first two miles of Walk 1. Paths can, in certain circumstances, be re-routed. This book gives details of the routes as we found them in 1993-1995. One thing to bear in mind is that some areas are prone to flooding. This is mentioned in the walks where we are aware of it, but you may encounter a flood elsewhere. If in doubt, allow even more time after wet weather.

Do not go out ill-prepared for the conditions. Stout footwear is essential on all of the walks in this booklet. Take with you warm, weatherproof clothing, especially on the more exposed routes or in the cooler months. In summer, always carry something to drink and use a sun block cream. If you have a mobile phone, take that with you too - it may save your life should you fall and break a limb. Please refer to the comments at the start of each walk. These give an indication of the degree of difficulty. An estimate of the time required, not allowing for breaks, is also shown at the top right of each walk (between the miles and kilometres figures).

Please observe the Country Code which, basically, means leave things as you find them. It is best if you leave no evidence of where you have been. Dogs can now go free on the train but, please control them in the countryside. If you stop for a picnic, take **all** your litter home with you. Tin cans, plastic bags etc. can kill farm animals.

Much of the walk is clearly waymarked. There are places, however, where the route may not be very apparent. Do not worry. Generally speaking, even with the introduction of the Criminal Justice Act, individual walkers cannot be prosecuted for trespass if they accidentally deviate from the official path, except in a few specific circumstances (e.g. on railway or Ministry of Defence property), but the land owner can sue if you cause damage to his property. Most land owners will be happy to steer you back to the correct path should you accidentally stray from it.

Intermediate distances are given in miles and tenths of a mile. If you prefer them in kilometres, then multiply the miles figure by about 1.6. In reverse, one kilometre is approximately 1100 yards (0.62 of a mile). The following conversion table may help.

Miles	Metres	Miles	Metres	Miles	Kms.
0.1	161	0.8	1287	6.0	9.656
0.2	322	0.9	1448	7.0	11.265
0.3	483	1.0	1609	8.0	12.875
0.4	644	2.0	3219	9.0	14.484
0.5	805	3.0	4828	10.0	16.093
0.6	966	4.0	6437	11.0	17.702
0.7	1127	5.0	8047	12.0	19.312

The walks contain references to various types of gate. A "wicket gate" means a small gate, usually alongside a larger one. A "kissing gate" is one which swings between two angled fences *(see top photo on page 30)*. To get through you push it away from you, move into the angle, then swing it back.

Arrows are sometimes used instead of text, so that, when holding the book parallel to the ground, you will have a better idea of the direction in which you should head. They are often followed by some object towards which you should aim.

↑ = Go straight ahead.   K = Go half-left
← = Turn left.   ↗ = Go half-right
→ = Turn right.

We occasionally mention places where refreshments may be available. It should be emphasised that these were taken purely from observation and it is in no way a recommendation. Public Houses will only be open during normal licensing hours and may not always have food available. Page 58 and the inside back cover give a directory of places through which the various walks pass. This directory also gives coded details of the types of facilities available. Often, some form of food (sandwiches etc.) can be purchased at village shops or Post Offices or even the local petrol station.

Most stations on the Hereford to Oxford railway line are served by direct trains from London Paddington, Slough and Reading. There are trains to Oxford from Gatwick Airport, the South Coast and the north. Worcester provides connections to/from South Wales, Gloucester, Cheltenham and Birmingham and Nottingham. Hereford is also host to trains to/from South Wales as well as to Shrewsbury and the north west of England. All except Worcester Foregate Street, Ascott-under-Wychwood, Finstock and Combe have car parking facilities, free of charge at the smaller ones.

The Cotswold Line Promotion Group, which exists to encourage the fullest use of the Hereford to Oxford line, hopes that you will enjoy trying out some of the walks in this booklet - and using our trains. If you have any comments on, or corrections/updates to, any of the walks, please write to the C.L.P.G. at 4, Sandford Rise, Charlbury, Oxford. OX7 3SZ. Copies of the current railway timetable for the Cotswold and Malvern Line and details of membership of the C.L.P.G. can be obtained from this address. Please send a stamped DL size (11cm x 22cm) envelope with details of your requirements.

Cover Photo: A "Thames Turbo" train alongside **Walk number 10**, near Ascott-under-Wychwood
We love to go a wandering,
Beside the railway track.
A cheery wave, to the train we gave,
That we need to take us back.
The photographs in this book were taken by John Stanley, unless otherwise stated.

The beginning and the end of the series of station-to-station walks.
Number 1 starts at Hereford *(above)* and **Number 12** ends at Oxford *(below)* and it is a case of the ancient and the modern. The main buildings at Hereford are historic, having originally been built in the mid 1800's as a large country residence, known as Barrs Court and are subject to a preservation order, whereas those at Oxford were constructed as recently as 1990. The complete walk between these two stations involves just less than 120 miles by the shortest of the routes described.

1 HEREFORD to LEDBURY

Ordnance Survey 1:50000 series map 149.

18.4 miles
9 hours
29.6 kms.

Hereford is an ancient cathedral city set alongside the River Wye. It has a modern city-centre with pedestrianised area and shopping precinct. There is a market hall and the centre contains most of the "national" stores. The Tourist Information Office is next to the Cathedral. The railway station has recently been refurbished and has a smart appearance. *A buffet is on the main platform.* Our first walk, which is the longest of the series due to the lack of intermediate stations, starts at Hereford railway station. There may be a convenient place for an overnight stop around the half way point. The Butchers Arms at Woolhope advertises Bed and Breakfast. As there are only three guest rooms, It may be best to telephone in advance to ensure that accommodation is available. ☎ (01432) 860281. There are some lengthy sections of walking along minor roads.

This is not one for the inexperienced walker as it may prove to be quite strenuous in parts and some places can be quite muddy. You will also be in the flood plain of the River Wye and River Lugg for part of it.

0.0   0.0   Leave the railway station and turn left opposite Safeway supermarket
(515406)   car park. Cross the main road and turn left. Over the railway bridge, take second road on right (Southbank Road) and continue along it when the main route (Bodenham Road) veers off to the right. At a T junction at the end of Southbank Road, go right on Folly Lane to a cross-roads. Go ↑, along Church Road, past a roadside cross (War Memorial) on your left. Continue ahead, eventually passing Hampton Dene Primary School, where the road name changes to Gorsty Lane.

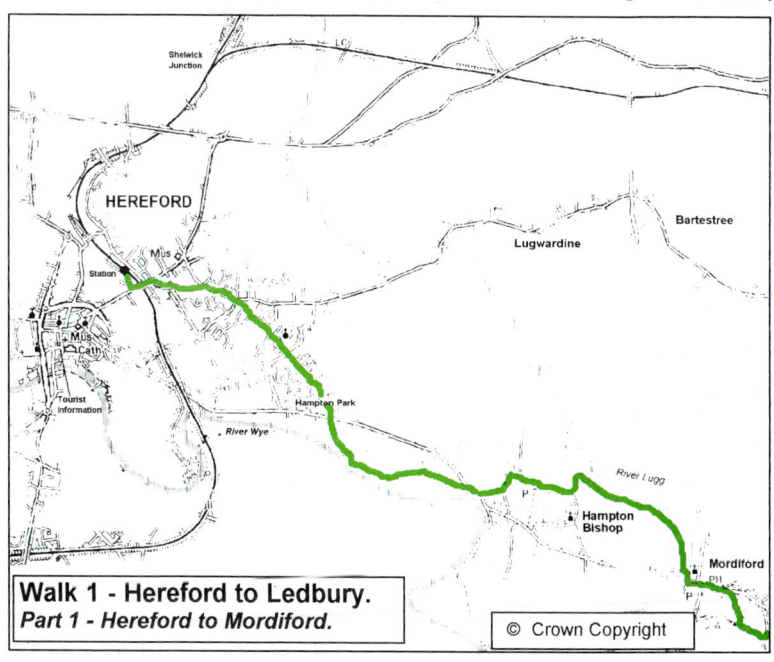

Walk 1 - Hereford to Ledbury.
Part 1 - Hereford to Mordiford.

© Crown Copyright

Turn left along Sudbury Avenue and continue on it until it ends at Hampton Park Road.

1.9   1.9   Go through a kissing gate opposite and follow waymarked "Wye Valley
(535391)   Walk", bearing slightly left over field to go through another kissing gate in fence near river bank. Cross next field ↗, to the river bank, continuing through four further kissing gates, then follow waymarker post to go ↖, across field, cross footbridge with stile at each end, then climb the flood bank. Go ➜, along bank top over two stiles, then ←, down steps and through gate into road.

1.1   3.0   Turn ➜, then, fifty yards on, beyond a telephone box at a lay-by, cross
(549383)   a stile in hedge left, then go ↑, to another at far side of field. Pass between houses to a lane and turn left, proceeding for half a mile through the village of **Hampton Bishop**. When the lane bears right, an unsignposted track diverges left. Take this to climb to the top of the flood bank of the River Lugg. Turn right and proceed along bank top through gateways to Mordiford Bridge. When close to the bridge, exit to the road by descending the bank, right, and climb stile.

1.8   4.8   Cross the nine-arch, 16th century, river bridge and enter the village.
(568375)   **Mordiford** grew up as an ancient ford over the River Lugg. The church, which dominates the end of the bridge, is of Norman origin but was much restored in the 19th century. When alongside Mordiford Post Office *(snacks and provisions available)* follow waymarkers along farm track right over stream then left to road. Cross road (Moon Inn to left) and go along driveway of Mill House following "Wye Valley Walk" markers through gate, farmyard and field to stile. When over, go slightly left, ascending the left hand of two fields (orchards), keeping close to hedge on right, to stile at end. Cross and proceed uphill, along a sunken path to a farm track by some cottages. Follow the waymarker ahead as far as cross tracks at Hope Springs Farm.

1.0   5.8   At this point, the Wye Valley Walk goes right. Our route turns left for
(577368)   some 25 yards then takes the right fork ascending to a road. Turn right along road for 200 yards, then take an access track to the left, climbing into Haugh Wood. Just past a modern cottage on the right, the main track veers sharply right in front of a barn.

1.4   7.2   At this point, a waymarker post points ahead to left of the barn. The
(586370)   path is a little overgrown at first, but keep to the edge of the woods with a field fence to the right. When the fence ends at a gateway, turn half right following a waymarker post and climb through wood. Ignore all side turnings. The path ends by a short "scramble" up a steep bank and onto a broad forestry track. Keep same heading to cross tracks where a wooden memorial bench offers a welcome rest opportunity. Keep ahead to a second cross track, where, go forward along a lesser used track for just over half a mile until it exits from the wood at a wooden barrier. Squeeze past the barrier with houses to the left and a

road is reached in a few yards.

1.0   8.2
(599363)
Turn ←, then, almost immediately take a right fork, signposted "Fownhope". After a half mile or so, in sight of a long, low factory-farm building to the right, follow a footpath sign, left, by a cattle grid going ↗, descending a field to the far side where a kissing gate admits to another field. Keep close to trees on your left and, after about 50 yards, go through trees by a small dam wall and turn right with the stream on the right, looking out for a kissing gate in the hedge on the left. Go through, and turning to right, walk around the field boundary to another kissing gate at the far corner. Having entered the adjacent field, follow the waymarker to cross field ↖, passing between two giant trees, with Woolhope church seen ahead. Go through a kissing gate onto lane and turn →. In a few yards, take a track, left, bending to right to enter the church yard by a gate.

1.0   9.2
(611358)
Proceed through the churchyard and into the road next to the Crown Inn (meals obtainable). Turn ← and straight away, → along a lane signposted to Putley and Ledbury, as far as the Butchers Arms public house at **Woolhope**. *(See introductory note regarding a break).*

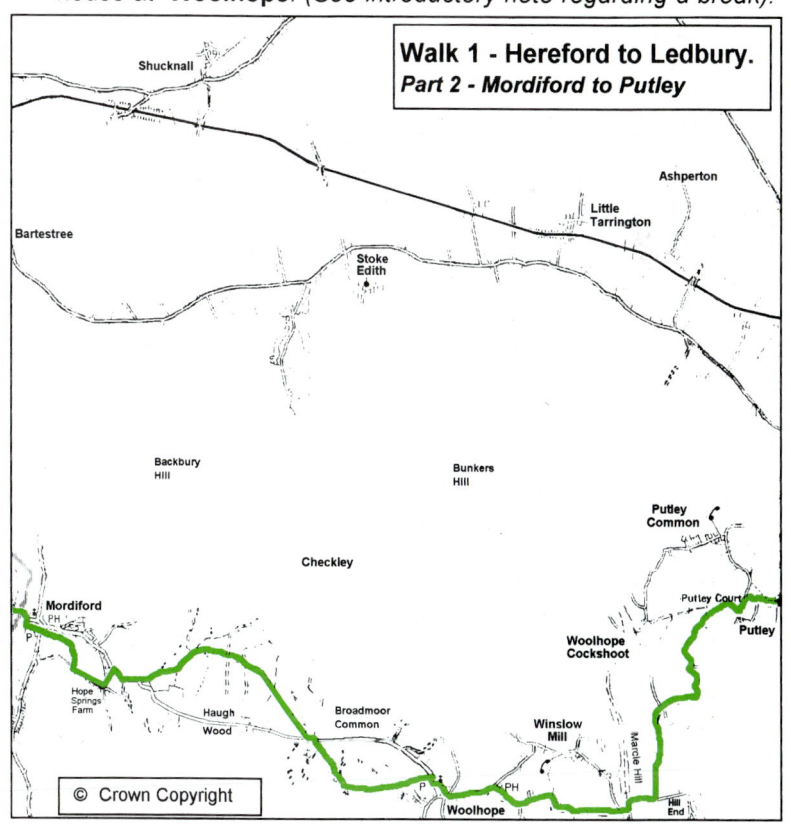

9

0.4   9.6   To continue the walk, follow farm drive on right in front of pub car park.
(617357)   After around 500 yards, continue ahead, ignoring left fork, going steeply uphill between hedges ending at a field gate just beyond a cottage to the right. Enter field and continue to climb across it, then descend to a stile at the left-hand corner of a wood. Go down hill inside wood on a clear path. At bottom, go through a gate by a stile, and, keeping hedge to your left, cross field to a gate at far corner. Go along a track between hedges, climbing to lane on the ridge top of Marcle Hill.

1.0   10.6   Cross lane and take track, left past a cottage, shortly descending
(631354)   steeply. The Malvern Hills come into view ahead, forming a backdrop to Ledbury and the spire of its parish church. In around 500 yards, go left at a junction, then, when you reach a crossroads, continue forward for around half a mile to a junction. Bear left, climbing to a junction of lanes by a cottage.

1.5   12.1   Turn right descending, with a good view of May Hill on the edge of the
(636373)   Forest of Dean and its distinctive clump of trees on the summit. Also, on a clear day, you can see the Cotswold escarpment behind. At next junction, go left for 100 yards, then turn → along a lane to a farmyard. Go through a gate ahead into a field, then, shortly ← through a wicket gate into Putley churchyard. Go towards the church then turn → to far end and enter field by a wicket gate. Go ↑ across field towards cottages, through a gate, along a track then forward along lane into **Putley Green** village.

1.1   13.2   By the Post Office (which is also the village shop), turn → and then ←
(652376)   at a lane junction (signposted to Aylton). *We could find no trace of a footpath, which is shown on the Ordnance Survey map, running direct from Putley Green to Aylton.* Bear right at a junction just beyond **Aylton** church. This leads, in about 600 yards, to the A4172 road.

1.0   14.2   Cross road and go through gate opposite. Cross paddock to a wicket
(664380)   gate, then over a grassy area at the side of a house to a further wicket gate. After passing through, go right, through a gateway, into the adjoining field. Go ahead, contouring around the slope and heading for a broad and high hedgerow. Ascend the next field with the hedge to your left and enter Ast Wood at the far end. About 25 yards inside the wood, go through a gateway and maintain the same general direction through the wood. There are many diverging paths, so it is important to always remain in sight of the edge of the wood to your left. After about a quarter of a mile, the edge of the wood is reached at a field corner. Go over a low wooden stile (supported underneath by old tyre covers at the time of the survey) and cross to far side of the field. Go over a stile next to a gate, under a wire fence and then diagonally across the next field to a gate. Pass through and go ← along a narrow lane to a junction, where turn →.

2.0   16.2   Go along lane for almost a mile until you reach a cottage named

(687377)   "Golden Grove" on the left. Go over the stile into a field/orchard, following the direction indicated by a finger post. Keep the fence close to your right. Pass between the fruit sheds and to the right of a bungalow, then bear right down a slope, aiming to the left of a pond at the bottom. Locate a stile in the hedge at a corner next to a large tree. Cross and go through the next field, keeping close to the fence on your left, to a gate leading into an adjacent field. At the far side of the gate, bear slightly right to traverse a large field, taking bearings from a factory on the sky-line with a very conspicuous brightly painted door. Cross a stile and a footbridge, go over by-pass to another footbridge. Having crossed over, bear left around a field to a wire fence around the Viking Packaging factory. The path passes between the hedge and the fence and then emerges into a field. Keeping the hedge to your right, go across two fields, with a view of the railway viaduct to the left. Becoming enclosed again, the path continues past a school to a road.

1.4 17.6 You now have a choice. If you wish to go straight to the station, you
(706380) will probably find it more pleasant, and interesting, to climb a low embankment to the left of the pedestrian footbridge spanning the road. You are now on the track formation of the former railway line which ran from Ledbury to Gloucester. The local council has taken over the section on the outskirts of Ledbury and converted it into an attractive footpath, well used by local residents. Turn left along the embankment and continue along it, passing the first exit (white rails on right) but taking a similar descent to the left shortly afterwards, looking for white handrails in the trees. This leads into a field. Continue in the same direction until you emerge onto the A438 next to a bungalow. Turn right, go under skewed bridge and follow road to T junction almost opposite entrance to Ledbury station where the
0.8 18.4 walk ends. (Grid reference 709386)

Walk 1 - Hereford to Ledbury.
Part 3 - Putley to Ledbury

© Crown Copyright

If you wish to visit **Ledbury** town centre, turn right at Grid reference 706380, go over the footbridge and along the old railway formation, until you reach the next road (Bye Steet). Turn left and in about 600 yards emerge into High Street in the town centre. There are plenty of facilities here, the Tourist Information Office is off to the left of the old Market House (a half timbered building on stilts) along a narrow alley called Church Lane. Public Conveniences are in the same area. There are numerous shops in Ledbury, including some of the larger "nationals". There are also several cafés. In fact, it would be a very pleasant town, were it not for the considerable amount of traffic which it seems to attract, despite the building of the bypass, crossed earlier.

Ledbury station is situated on the right, about 900 yards along Homend, the road to your left when you entered the town centre. This detour will extend the walk to a total of around 19 miles.

Church Lane, Ledbury looking towards the town centre. Note the cobbled footway and the half-timbered buildings. This lane is on a suggested detour from **Walk 2** but can also be visited on **Walks 1 and 2A**.
Photo: Bob Brown.

2 LEDBURY to COLWALL

Ordnance Survey 1:50000 series map 149 & 150.

Ledbury is a pleasant "black and white" Herefordshire market town, half a mile or so from the station.   It is best visited either at the end of walk 1 from Hereford (where more details are given) or at the start of the alternative, but much longer walk (2A) to Colwall via Eastnor. The walk described below goes away from the town, although glimpses of it can be seen in the distance below, if you look back after you have walked three quarters of a mile or so. Alternatively, you may turn left along the road on leaving station, and, after visiting the town centre, make for the parish church via the cobbled Church Lane *(see photograph on opposite page)*. Just inside church yard take the left path which exits between high brick walls and leads to Church Street. Continue ahead until it turns sharp left. Here, ascend a series of shallow steps to a steep sunken track up to a wood. At a junction of tracks, take the right hand one which soon levels out and becomes a very pleasant route, at the fringe of mature woodland and enables you to join the main route at point 0.6 (715386) below.   Go straight across road following lane for 200 yards to farm. The actual walk starts at Ledbury station.

Other than for a few steep climbs, this is not a strenuous walk. Some paths could be quite muddy, especially in rainy periods.

If you are planning a full day's walk, you may wish to consider proceeding straight on from Walk 2 to Walk 3 - Colwall to Great Malvern.

0.0   0.0   From Ledbury station, turn right at end of driveway and follow road
(709386)   under railway bridge. Almost immediately after bridge, climb a stile on right (waymarked) into a field.   Keep close to the wire fence on your right and ascend over stiles through two further fields, then through a kissing gate on to a driveway. Go forward to the road, noting a view of Ledbury station below, through trees to the right. At the road junction, turn left up hill for 300 yards.

0.6   0.6   Take left turn for 200 yards, bearing left at a footpath sign into a farm
(715386)   yard. Immediately turn right between two hedges, then through the right hand of two gates into a field. Climb steep field keeping hedge on your left then enter a wood by a stile.   Go forward over a small rise, then turn left when you join a wider path.

0.3   0.9   Follow this path for about 400 yards, then climb left, up a narrow path
(716389)   through the trees, turning right onto the ridge top path. This eventually starts to gradually descend. At a fork, bear left, then left again at second fork, until you cross the main forestry track. Look for a stile opposite with a **"CW57"** marker alongside. Climb over this stile and follow path through pleasant woodland. You will emerge into a field at which point you turn half-left and aim for a gate in the bottom left hand corner.

1.1   2.0   Go left along lane for a third of a mile or so until you reach the entrance
(723405)   to **Hope End Hotel** on right just beyond a cutting. Go through gate to the left of the main driveway and cross rising field aiming for two large

13

trees at the top. Once over the brow, aim for the **far** left corner of the field, passing to the left of a walled garden, then keeping to the right of a wood. Go over a stile and follow track between two fences. Where the left hand fence veers left, keep following the right hand one to the trig point at the top of **Oyster Hill** (691 feet above sea level).   An excellent view of the surrounding countryside can be obtained from here and it is a good location for a break or picnic if the weather is fine. The official right of way is below and to the left of the trig point but there is now little evidence of where it should be, as common usage seems to have "diverted" it to the right.

1.0   3.0   Continue in the same direction then descend steep path. Cross track,
(723418)   then go over stile in iron railing fence (on your left if you are following the official right of way).   Head straight on, over several stiles, to emerge to the left of a house on to a road.

0.5   3.5   Turn ➜ along road for 25 yards then ⬅ along a road signposted
(731423)   Colwall and Malvern. In half a mile, when road bends left, enter church yard by a gate. Colwall Parish Church is dedicated to St. James the Great, and has a small "Ale House", built to encourage the locals to attend church.   It is now used for social functions.

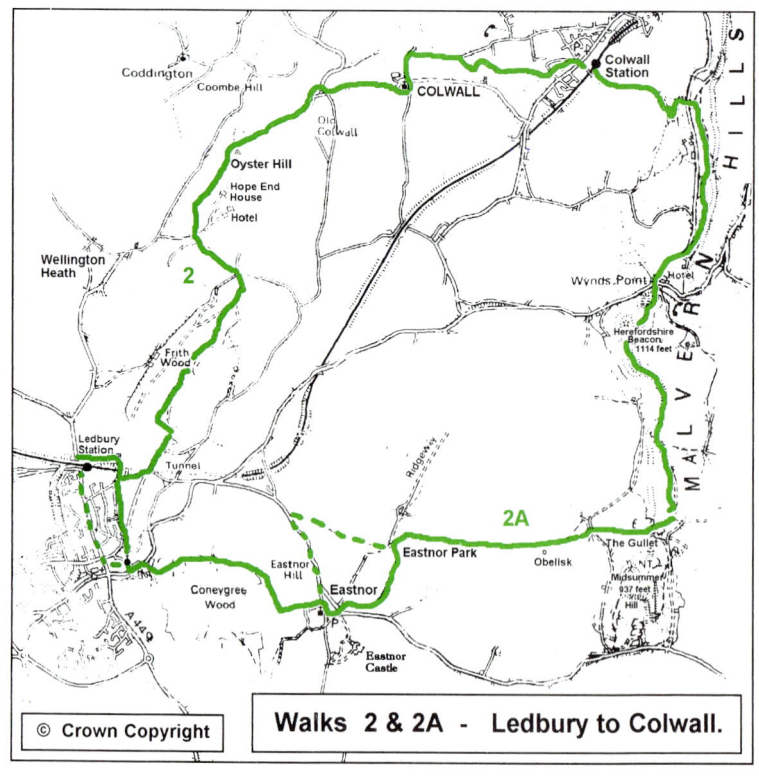

Walks 2 & 2A - Ledbury to Colwall.

© Crown Copyright

14

0.7 4.2 Exit through the gate next to the Ale House, turn **left** and follow road
(739423) for a hundred yards to a road junction. Cross to a gate and stile
opposite. Go along an access track through a belt of trees until you
reach a cattle grid. By-pass the grid by a gate on the left, then
immediately turn ➜, following field boundary to your right. Pass
through a kissing gate into a lane, then maintain the same direction
until you reach a black and white cottage. Immediately before this
cottage, go through a kissing gate on the right, then cross a small field
keeping close to a hedge on the left. Go though a second kissing gate,
cross to the far side of the next field, through yet another kissing gate,
then turn ⬅ around the edge of a large field. At end of field, follow
path round to the right. About half way along the hedge is a kissing
gate. Go through this, aim ⬈ for another kissing gate, then follow track
into Colwall Stone village. At road, keep straight on, past Colwall
Royal British Legion Club until you reach main road, by the Post
Office. Cross main road. Colwall station is just behind the Colwall
1.3 5.5 Park Hotel at Grid Reference 757425.

2A LEDBURY to COLWALL

via Eastnor Park

Ordnance Survey 1:50000 series maps 149 & 150.

9.5 miles
6 hours
15.3 kms.

**For the benefit of those wanting something longer or more strenuous
(Ledbury station is about 250 feet above sea level, whereas the summit of
the Herefordshire Beacon is at 1114 feet), this walk is offered as an
alternative to Walk number 2.   The route map is on page 14 (opposite).**

0.0 0.0 From Ledbury railway station, exit along the drive, turning sharp ➜ at
(709386) the road. Go under the railway bridge and, almost immediately, climb
stile to right (yellow waymark) ascending three fields via two further
stiles, always keeping close to wire fence on the right. Go through a
kissing gate into a driveway.

0.5 0.5 Keep forward along drive to a road, noting a view of Ledbury station
(712387) through the trees to your right. Cross to the opposite side and climb
the steps into a wood. Follow the main path, keeping to the edge of
the wood, with the rear to a house to the right. Ignore a broad left
turning at the end of the wood and continue forward on a steeply
descending sunken track and steps to a road at the bottom of the hill.
Proceed ⬆, after 50 yards taking path between high brick walls to the
left, emerging in Ledbury Parish Churchyard.

0.5 1.0 Turn to left in front of church and pass by the detached early 14th
(713377) century bell-tower, following the path round the main church building,
emerging via path onto main road. Turn ⬅ and, after 100 yards, cross
road and enter wood by a path at a signpost indicating "L.16, L.17" TO

EASTNOR. The path, keeping to the edge of a wood, climbs to a bridle gate. Pass through and, straight away, take a narrow path ↖, ascending steeply. Cross a forestry track and continue to climb to a second track.

0.5   1.5   Turn ← along track for 25 yards then →, along a path and through
(717377)   bridle gate into a field.   Turn ← along field boundary, continuing to the far corner, where you cross a stile and proceed ahead into a further field, once again keeping hedge to your left.   Cross a stile at far end and enter a wood.   Immediately, turn ← and, via a stile, enter field, proceeding around the edge of wood with the hedge on your right. When reaching a gate into the wood, turn ← in front of it, crossing the field, passing close to two stunted trees and go through gateway, climbing a short slope to the crest of a ridge.   Descend ↖ across field with Eastnor church directly ahead.   Pass through two wicket gates, across a further field with hedge to the right, to the far end, descending steps cut into the bank.   Exit onto road through wicket gate, turn → and you will soon reach the lych-gate entrance to Eastnor churchyard.

1.1   2.6   Continue along road, bearing left past the school and the village Post
(731371)   Office (which is housed, delightfully, in a timber framed thatched cottage).   Note the main entrance to Eastnor Castle on the right. Cross the A483 main road and proceed ahead along driveway past a saw mill.

The rather forbidding notices on this drive are directed to the drivers or riders of wheeled vehicles. We have been in touch with the Estate Office at Eastnor who have confirmed that they do not to object to walkers using this route to gain access to the footpath to the obelisk. However, they have requested that we point out that the land over which this path passes is private property and, therefore, may be closed to the public on occasions when special events are taking place. In this case, it will be necessary to turn left and walk 0.6 mile along the main A483 road until you reach the official footpath on the right.   This will add about a mile to your journey.   You then rejoin the walk as described at point ♦ , continuing straight on downhill.

Go over a cattle-grid and enter parkland, always keeping close to fence on the left.   When   drive reaches crest of the ridge, look out for a gateway and yellow waymarker on the left. ♦ When at this point, turn sharp → (no waymarker) descending steeply over grass, between two ponds in valley bottom, to a rough track.   In summer, this area is used as a camping site.   Upon the descent, an obelisk at the top of the hill opposite is in view. You should now aim for this.   Cross the track and climb the hill, following various vehicle tracks; the result of four-wheel-drive rallying. After just over ½ mile, the obelisk is reached.

1.8   4.4   *The 90 foot high structure was erected in memory of distinguished*
(752378)   *members of the Seymour-Cocks family of Eastnor Castle and can be a*

16

convenient place to stop for a break.

From here, descend along a clear track to a black metal wicket gate. On the far side of the gate, three tracks join. Take the forward, descending, track through a pretty wooded valley called "The Gullet" between Swinyard and Midsummer Hills (almost at the southern extremity of the Malvern Hills range). A disused quarry in the side of Swinyard Hill comes into view on the left. Opposite here, bear left between four squat stone bollards, alongside a pool and on a lane to a road junction on the edge of Castlemorton Common.

0.9   5.3   Take a sharp ← turn here. This will lead up Swinyard Hill. Keep
(765381)   following the footpath which will take you over Hangman's Hill and to the top of the Herefordshire Beacon. In fine weather, this part of the walk will offer you fine views to left and right. There is an Iron Age hill fort on the Beacon. You then descend to the A449 road at the Malvern Hills Hotel, which is open all year round, providing meals and accommodation. In summer there is a kiosk, opposite, offering take-away refreshments. Public toilets are alongside. If the weather is not so fine, you may prefer to keep to a lower level by following pathways around the back of the hills to rejoin the route at the Hotel.

1.6   6.9   Take the road, signposted "West Malvern", around a bend to a small
(763404)   car park. At the far end of the car park, a track gently ascends the hillside, keeping sight of the road. When a bifurcation occurs, take the narrow path through trees to the left and, ignoring any divergences (falling or rising) to left or right, emerge at another roadside car park. Exit to the road and cross by a sign to "The Kettle Sings Cafe". Go straight downhill over an area of rough grass to the cafe, which is a low red-tile roofed building. *It is open daily, all year round, excepting Tuesdays from November to February. Being only some twenty minutes from the end of the walk, it may be a useful refreshment stop.*

1.5   8.4   Turn ← in front of the cafe and go downhill on a path through trees to a
(765422)   stile on the right. Climb over and go along a clear path around the edge of a field, bending to the left and a stile at the bottom. When over this, continue straight down the hill to a small belt of trees. Aim for a large holly tree, slightly to the right, and take a narrow diagonally sloping path under it. Zig-zag down a steep slope to a stile between a fence and a hedge. Climb stile, then cross field, with hedge close on the right, to a gate at the far end. Go through the gate and, 25 yards along the track ahead is a railway footbridge. Go over this and you will
1.1   9.5   arrive at the platform of Colwall station (757425) - the end of the walk.

If you are feeling particularly energetic, you may continue to Great Malvern by combining this walk with number 3 and continuing straight on at the Kettle Sings Cafe (765422). This will bring you up onto the ridge path which is later joined by Walk number 3 at grid reference 769427. Follow the instructions for that walk from this reference.

3 COLWALL to MALVERN

Ordnance Survey 1:50000 series map 150.

4.1 miles
2.5 hours
6.6 kms.

The Malvern Hills which are maintained by the Malvern Hills Conservation Trust, are made up from a long narrow ridge of ancient Pre-Cambrian rocks, which tower dramatically over the Worcestershire Plain. The highest point is the Worcestershire Beacon, at 1394 feet. From the summit, on a clear day, there are excellent views to the East, over the Severn Valley, Vale of Evesham and the Cotswold Escarpment. This contrasts with the rolling countryside to the West, which rises up to the Black Mountains in Wales. To the North are the Shropshire hills and the Black Country. The Pre-Cambrian rocks (slates and granite) are much harder than the younger, softer, overlying strata which has been eroded away to expose the steep sided ridge. The Walk starts from Colwall railway station.

This walk involves a gradual ascent of almost 1000 feet. The descent to Malvern is much steeper. Refreshments are available at St Ann's Well, at various cafes in Malvern and at Great Malvern railway station.

0.0 0.0 Cross over the footbridge and onto the path. At a kissing gate, follow
(757425) the sign "Worcestershire Way". Keep left along the edge of the field, over the stile and turn left, following the hedge. Before a barn, cut right by some trees, to follow the edge of the field up a gentle slope, to reach a gate at top left. Take the track which goes through the gate, keeping right where it forks, through another gate, to join a tarmac lane going in the same direction.

0.9 0.9 At the road junction, take the grassy path on the right, which ascends
(767432) the slope past some houses. The path crosses another road and a path as it climbs steadily up the ridge.

0.3 1.2 On the ridge, turn left, heading North. The ridge path drops slightly to
(769427) cross the road, by a shelter and toilets.

0.2 1.4 Continue by following up Beacon Road, where a path leads off on the
(769437) right shortly afterwards. This continues up to the summit of Worcestershire Beacon (1394 feet above sea level).

0.9 2.3 From the summit, take one of the grassy paths on the right (Malvern)
(769452) side, which rejoin the ridge path.

0.5 2.8 Where the path crosses the head of a steep valley, take the path to
(767461) the right which winds down into the valley. At the junction with a track, descend via a steep grassy path to the stream and follow it down into Great Malvern passing St Ann's Well on the way.

0.6 3.4 At the town centre, turn →, bear left (post office on the right) down the
(775460) hill and follow the sign to **Great Malvern** railway station where the
0.7 4.1 walk ends at Grid Reference 783457. Alternatively, you can make a detour using one of several paths through Priory Park. Exit next to the Splash Leisure Complex. Cross car park ↗ then take road ←. When you see a railway bridge ahead, turn ←. The station is on the right.

18

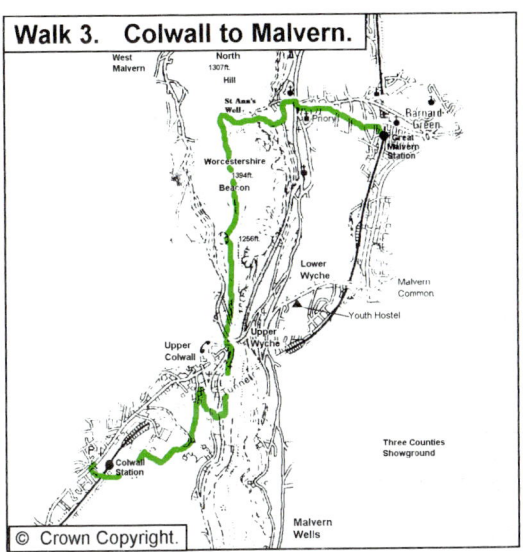

Walk 3. Colwall to Malvern.

West Malvern

North Hill 1307ft.

St Ann's Well

Priory

Barnard Green

Great Malvern Station

Worcestershire 1394ft. Beacon

1256ft.

Lower Wyche

Malvern Common

Youth Hostel

Upper Colwall

Upper Wyche

Three Counties Showground

Colwall Station

Malvern Wells

© Crown Copyright.

Below:

Walks 2A and 3 both involve climbing to the top of part of the Malvern Hills. In the foreground of this general view, taken from **Walk number 2A,** looking north, is the British Camp, an Iron Age fortress on the Herefordshire Beacon. This walk then proceeds along the ridge top before descending to Colwall. **Walk number 3** joins the ridge about half way along and proceeds into the distance, passing over the highest point on the hills, The Worcestershire Beacon, in the process.

Photo: • Derek Potter.

19

Malvern owes its existence to the Victorian health craze of the 19th century and its relatively sheltered position on the eastern side of the massive Malvern Hills, from which oozes the famous mineral water - now sold in bottles all over the world. It is an elegant place, reminiscent of other Spa towns like Buxton or Leamington, but having that unique quality and charm of its own. It boasts a priory church, the tower of which dominates the town and, nearby, some lovely gardens. It looks as though Malvern once tried to climb the hills, with various housing developments clinging to the steep slopes, but, in more modern times, it has slipped down a little and it is now spreading over the flat plains to the east.

This is a relatively easy walk as the countryside through which it passes is either rolling hills or riverside plains. Do not attempt the final part in particularly wet weather as the Teme and the Severn are both liable to overflow their banks. You should be able to walk along the road from Powick into Worcester unless it has been exceptionally wet.

Malvern has two railway stations (it used to have four) so we have had to decide from which one to start the walk. This was not an easy decision, so we have avoided making it. We will start from both!

Great Malvern station originates from the opening of the line in 1860. It was extensively damaged by fire in the early 1980's but was restored to something like its former glory in 1986. It now boasts a delightful, privately run, refreshment room, so why not pop in for a coffee before you set out on your walk.

0.0 0.0 Leave the station and cross diagonally right the grassed area, with
(775460) trees, opposite. Aim for the far corner at a cross roads. Go straight across into what is a continuation of Imperial Road, noting the dome shaped building, surrounded by water in the grounds of the school to your right. When you come to a T junction, turn ←, cross Tibberton Road then take the next turning on the right (Albert Road North). Continue past the Manor Park Club and turn → down the driveway next to the Malvern Hills College of Adult Education (footpath sign).

0.4 0.4 Follow the pathway which bears left off the driveway. Pass an
(779462) apparently disused stile then continue, ↖, across a field and descend to a stile near to the bottom left hand corner. Cross this and a small stream then go through trees with wood panel fencing on your left. When you reach the end of a residential cul-de-sac, turn, →, and go under the railway line. Immediately, take the left fork and follow the path between two fences/hedges until you emerge into a field. ✂ To go to Malvern Link, turn, ←, and aim for gap in the hedge. Go through archway of bushes, the path leading to a small residential area. Cross grass and go down passageway opposite. Keep straight on where another path joins, passing a school on your right. Keep following the path until you reach another residential area. Ignore turning to your left and keep almost straight on up an incline. When just over the brow,

take a footpath up some steps, between the houses on your left. Follow path round to the right and keep straight on where the track turns left (i.e. do not cross the railway). Head for a bench then, descend a steep grassy bank. Cross track and go up opposite side. After passing through some trees, turn ←, then → and cross the Common to Malvern Link station, which is on the opposite side of Worcester Road. You can shorten the walk by continuing ↑ across field at ✂ above and along road. At traffic lights, go straight on and

0.9   1.3   follow road until just before a roundabout. Turn → at point ✿ below.

Malvern Link station, unfortunately, fell victim to the demolition men, having been similar in many ways to Great Malvern, but is now just a cabin on one side and a waiting room on the other, although the old station house remains - in private occupation. Nevertheless, the staff take care of their station and, in spring, the banks of daffodils are delightful.

0.0   0.0   Leave the station and turn ← down the main road. There are public
(783476)   toilets on the left, just before the junction (opposite) with Pickersleigh Road. Continue along the main road, past the shops - there is a restaurant and a fish and chip shop among them - until you reach a cross roads with a set of traffic lights.

0.2   0.2   Turn →, (Pickersleigh Avenue) and continue until you reach a phone
(786477)   box, where you turn ←, (SP to Industrial Estate). If you wish, you could have cut diagonally, across Victoria Park, but this may not be recommended if the two football pitches are in use!   Just before you reach a T junction, turn right and continue straight on to the right of Malvern R.F.C. Having passed the pitches, go over a stile at the end then turn ←. When you reach a cross-path, turn ← through gateway then immediately → to follow hedge on your right. You will eventually emerge via a stile onto a road. ✿ Go straight across and follow path, aiming for a stile in the hedge. This leads to a lane.

1.00   1.2   Go straight across and along Rectory Lane. After about 400 yards, you
(798473)   will pass a large house on the left. Look for a little-used stile next to a gate on the left. Go over this, then cross field, ↗, to a footbridge over a stream with stiles at each end. Continue on same heading across next field, leaving by a gate in the left corner. Immediately go over a stile on the right and cross the next field, aiming to the left of the houses on the far side.   This emerges, via a stile, to the village of **Madresfield**. Note the rather attractive church, dedicated to St. Mary the Virgin.

0.6   1.8   Turn left along the road then, after about 50 yards, follow footpath sign
(804476)   to the right along Tarmac path into the grounds of Madresfield Court. At fork, bear right then go under two bridges. The driveway then turns sharp right. Go straight on through a kissing gate, then, ignoring a waymarker pointing left, go ↑, across the large field you have just entered, aiming for a waymarked stile in the far left corner.   Go over

then, again, go straight on, ↑, skirting a wood at the points where it juts out into what are two adjacent fields. You should gradually aim for the end of the wood on your left. At this point, go through a gate on the left and over a stream. Cross the next field to the right hand corner where you go through a gate on the right. Immediately, go over a stile on the left and enter a pleasant woodland area. Follow the path, ignoring a cross-path until you leave the wood via a footbridge over a stream followed by a stile. Go straight across, ↑, field and over two stiles. Turn → and, shortly, go through a small gate in right-hand corner. This leads into a pleasant "common" area. Follow the path straight on up a hill, passing a trig point on your right.

1.3   3.1   This could be a good place for a picnic on a fine day. There are
(826487)   several benches on which to sit and there are good views both in front and behind. To continue, go down hill aiming for some houses on your left. Just before the first house, follow a track to the left and proceed round to the right, passing behind the houses. When past, bear left following a path to the left of a hill. Go over a stile, then straight on, ↑, keeping hedge on your right. At end of the field, go over stile onto a track/lane. Turn → and continue straight on to the main road in the village of **Callow End**. Turn ← and follow road past the Old Bush public house *(food advertised)* for about 300 yards until you reach a telephone box on the right.

0.8   3.9   Turn → and continue to the end of the road at T junction. Cross
(835496)   road to left then go through gate. Cross football pitches to stile on half-way line. Go over then head ↖, over next field, aiming for an electricity pylon. At the end of this field, turn ←, following hedge on your left towards a black and white house, emerging via an enclosed track onto a road.

0.5   4.4   Turn left, then immediately right, following footpath sign. Note the
(839500)   Abbey across the field to your left. Follow the track until it turns to the left. From here, a footpath crosses, ↖, the field on your right. Take this path and, at the end of the field, turn ← and go straight across field, heading just to the left of Powick Sewage Works ahead. Go over stile then straight on, following wire-mesh fence until it turns left. Here continue straight on across field to a stile. Go over, also crossing a stream. Go straight on to gate opposite, then keep to left side of hop-field, then orchard. Go through gates at end, cross track, go over stile and straight across small field. Go through a kissing gate into Powick church yard, following pathway in front of church. Keep straight on, leaving church yard by another kissing gate. Immediately, turn right down steps. At bottom, go over a stile/footbridge/stile then go half left across field. At far side you will emerge via a stile onto the very busy A449 road. Turn right, →, past the Vernon Arms public house *(hot and cold*

Above: Look to the right in the village of Cropthorne on **Walk number 6** and you will to see this attractive property, Holland House, now used by the Diocese of Worcester as a retreat house and conference centre.
Photo: Derek Potter.

Below: In the centre of Evesham is the attractive Market Place. The large half-timbered building is Booth Hall, erected in the 15th century and now occupied by National Westminster Bank. Evesham is featured in **Walks numbers 6 and 7** and you will cross this square if you take a suggested detour via the Abbey Park..

food advertised),cross road then take the next turn on the left. This leads to Powick old bridge over the river Teme.

On the left is Powick Mill. This was once the City of Worcester Electricity Works and, according to the notice board, was the first large scale hydro-electric power station in the world.

1.4 5.8 ■ From here, turn right, having crossed the bridge, and take the path
(835524) over a stile. Go under the left hand archway of the "new" bridge then follow the most pleasant riverside path alongside the River Teme. When you reach the fifth stile (the second of which had no fence alongside it when we researched the route), cut off a loop in the river by going half-left, ↖, across the next field to rejoin the river bank. Pass another disused stile and you will eventually reach the confluence of the River Teme with the River Severn an a point marked by a green signpost and some seats. Follow the pathway round to the left. When you reach the third stile, you will join a new footpath/cycleway.

■ *At the time of our research, (October 1994), the path was completely impassable where it passes under Powick new bridge, due to foul-smelling water/mud up to a foot deep! The matter has been reported to Worcester City Council and it would be worth checking whether this mess has been cleared, but, failing this, the alternative is to return to the old bridge and continue along the lane. When re-emerging onto the A449, continue in the same direction until you reach a small roundabout. Follow "City Centre" sign to the right (Bromwich Road). Take the second turn to the right (Weir Lane). Keep straight on at the end, along the new cycleway, and continue down to the River Severn. At this point the originally intended path from Powick Bridge joins from the right. Turn left.*

1.7 7.5 Follow the riverside path. There are plenty of benches along here on
(846531) which to rest if you are ahead of time. There are also some excellent views including Diglis Weir, with the locks behind, the latter perhaps being best viewed from Walk number 5, Diglis Oil Dock, the entrance to the Worcester and Birmingham canal and of Worcester Cathedral *(see photo on page 30)*. On the left is the Worcestershire County Cricket ground. When you reach the river bridge, cross over then continue along Bridge Street. You can reach **Worcester Foregate Street** station by taking the left fork into the pedestrianised area and turning left past the market stalls in Angel Place. Public toilets are available on the right. Turn right along Angel Street. At Foregate, turn left where you will see the station on your right about 200 yards ahead.

1.2 8.7 This is the end of the walk (849552).

If you wish to catch a train from Worcester's other station, **Shrub Hill**, keep ↑ when you reach the end of Angel Street. Continue ↑ (St Nicholas St.) until you reach a main road, with pedestrian crossing lights. Keep virtually ↑ along Lowesmoor. When over canal bridge, bear right. Shrub Hill station is on the left.

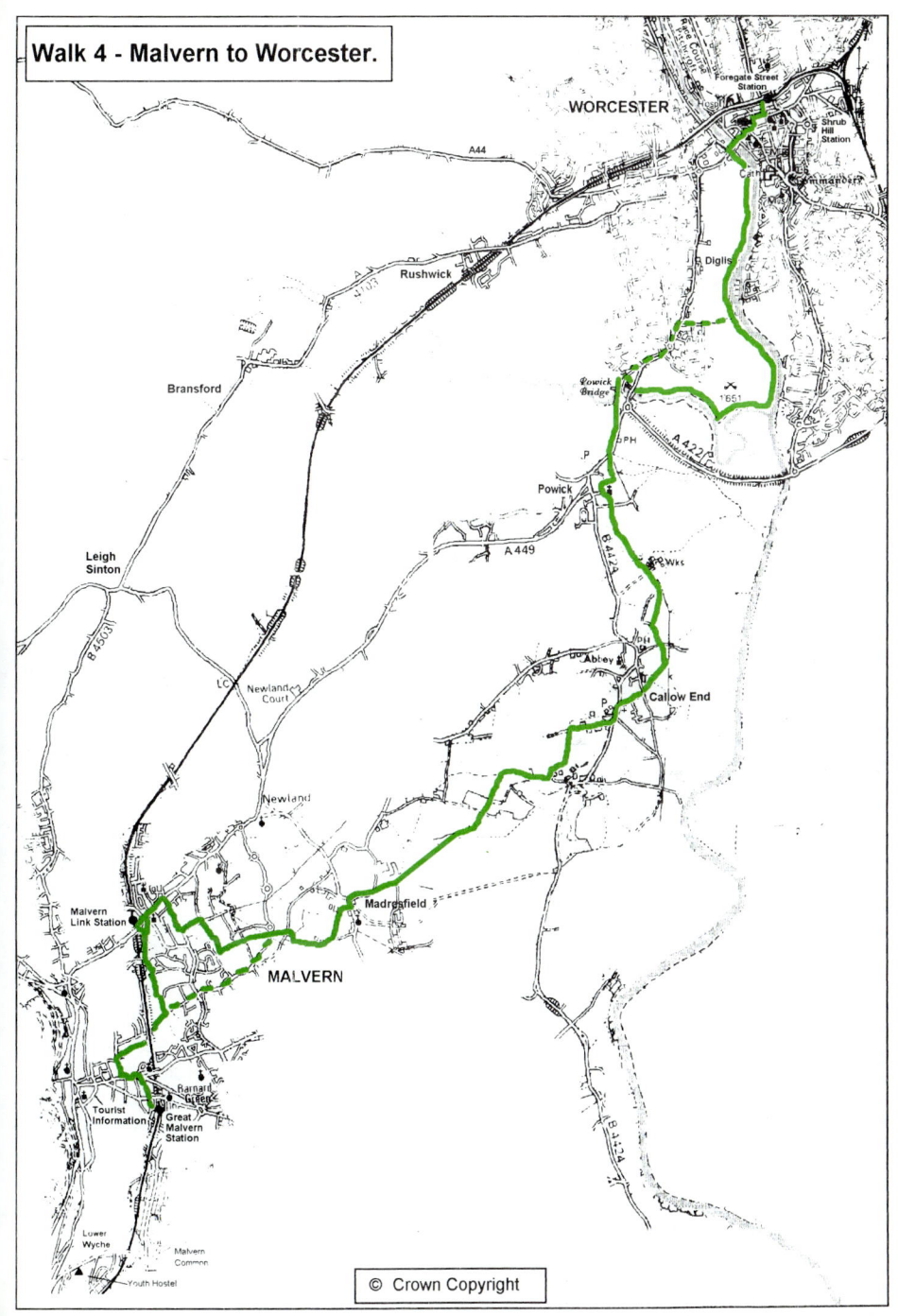

Walk 4 - Malvern to Worcester.

WORCESTER

Foregate Street Station

Shrub Hill Station

Diglis

A44

Rushwick

A 4103

Powick Bridge

1651

A 422

Bransford

P

PH

Powick

Leigh Sinton

A 449

B 4424

Wks

B 4503

PH

Abbey

Callow End

LC

Newland Court

P

Newland

Malvern Link Station

Madresfield

MALVERN

Tourist Information

Barnard Green

Great Malvern Station

Lower Wyche

Malvern Common

B 4424

Youth Hostel

© Crown Copyright

25

Worcester is an attractive city spanning the River Severn. As well as the Cathedral which dominates the skyline, there is an abundance of venues to attract the tourist. All the major stores are represented in the city centre and there are numerous smaller shops, especially in the historic little streets and passageways nearby. The Tourist Information Office is situated next to the Guildhall in High Street, just along from Foregate Street station, where our walk commences. However, if you wish to start from Worcester's other station (Shrub Hill), you may like to join the main walk at Diglis (♁, below) where the Worcester and Birmingham Canal joins the River Severn. To do this, leave the station, taking the left side of the approach road. Cross main road and go down Tallow Hill and round a left hand bend at the bottom. Do not cross the canal but join the tow-path just after the bridge. Follow tow-path past several locks and through the Diglis basin until you reach the river, where you turn left. You will pass the "Commandery" on your way *(refreshments available)*.

This is not a particularly strenuous walk, even though it is 50% longer than the train journey. Do not attempt it after long periods of heavy rain. You may get no further than Bridge Street in Worcester. South Quay can be under up to five feet of water and there will be swans swimming on it!

0.0   0.0   Starting from **Foregate Street** station *(light refreshments available)*,
(849552) turn ←, then take the second → along Angel Street. Turn first ← into Angel Place. If you require the public toilets, they are on your left. Continue straight on past the market stalls then turn → into Broad Street. At set of traffic lights by All Saints church, cross road and continue along Bridge Street down to the river.

0.4   0.4   Do not cross the river. Turn ← and follow the bankside path along
(847548) South Quay. Pass the Cathedral and continue until you reach the entrance to the Worcester and Birmingham canal ♁ which you cross by means of a wooden swing bridge. Continue on narrow path alongside the river and then cross Diglis Oil Dock by an inclined bridge to join a road. Turn and bear right along Diglis Road until you reach Diglis River Locks. Rejoin the riverside path past a signpost "Riverside Walk to Cherry Orchard".

1.1   1.5   The path now becomes unsurfaced, narrower and a little rough in
(847533) places. When it reaches a deep gully where a stream issues out into the River Severn, turn ← and look for a narrow plank footbridge to the right, to regain the river bank on the far side. Ignore all side turnings and eventually emerge into a caravan site. The vicinity is overshadowed by the massive concrete viaduct of the Worcester Southern Relief Road.

An interesting diversion may be made here. Walk under the bridge then look out for a narrow path climbing the bank to a stile to come out at a major road junction, next to a brick viewing platform. Climb the grassy bank to the top of the platform where there is a display board giving details of the Battle of Worcester, a decisive battle in the Civil War, which took place at several locations in this area on 3rd September 1651.

1.2   2.7   To resume the walk, retrace your steps to the river bank and continue
(853516)   through a small wood. The path gets a little rough in parts but soon comes out into a yacht club driveway. Go forward past the club house then over a stile and into a field. Keeping close to the river, a series of stiles will bring you into the village of **Kempsey**. When level with the parish church, go, ←, up a lane and through a wooden gate into the churchyard.

1.6   4.3   Walk straight across the churchyard, then go over a footbridge by a
(848491)   ford and up to the A38 road. Turn right here, past the Walter de Cantelupe Inn *(meals, lunchtimes and evenings)* taking the second left (Napleton Lane). Walk on past the houses, then take a stile by a cattle grid at a white gateway leading to Napleton House. At a second gateway, go over a stile, right, and along a field path to a footbridge. Go →, on a lane, bear left at a turn, then ← at the T junction to cross the M5 Motorway, noting a fine half-timbered thatched cottage alongside.

1.4   5.7   At the Farmer's Arms public house, go ahead through a gate along a
(865483)   track across **Kempsey** Common. At the top of the rise, go, ↖, towards a fence and to the right of a red brick farmhouse in the distance. Following the fence line, go through a gate, forking left then ahead on a lane past the Organ Grinder pub *(meals)* to Stonehall Common. At left turn, go sharp right on a path between gorse bushes across the common to a gate at the far side. Pass through and along a, sometimes muddy, bridleway to a road junction in **Littleworth**.

1.7   7.4   Go right for 100 yards, then turn ←, at a footpath sign, and, at the edge
(886495)   of a playing field, over a stile in the hedge, right, crossing a field to a fence alongside the railway line. Follow the fence to a stile next to the road bridge.   Turn left, crossing the railway, and left again at a T junction. In 200 yards, go through a gateway, along a field boundary with the hedge on your right, onto the road at the village of **Hawbridge**. There are bus stops here for Pershore or Worcester if required.

1.4   8.8   Turn right, then, in front of the Bird in Hand pub car park *(meals)*, cross
(906492)   road through kissing gate, cross field and stile then down to A44 road. Cross the road, going straight ahead, ↑, over rough ground and through a gap in the hedge and fence to turn ↗, over field to cross a small footbridge and stile. Go ← through a pasture towards a group of ancient willow trees, then over a stile and stream by a rather overgrown bridge. Follow the field boundary with the hedge on your left, then go over a stile into another field at the far side of which a gate admits to Windmill Hill Farm.

0.7   9.5   Go straight ahead and along driveway. Just past a left turn and in front
(916496)   of a cottage on right, cross a stile, right, through a field on a clear path
onto a road where you should turn ←. In a few yards, turn → at a
junction. Proceed ahead along the lane until just before the junction
with the A44 main road. Take a clearly signposted field path on the left
to **Drakes Broughton**, using the elegant spire of the parish church as
your marker. Go by the village school to a road junction in front of the
church. Proceed straight ahead on a pleasant country lane, crossing a
ford by a footbridge and turning left on the main road to reach Pershore
1.5 12.0   station (951480).

If you wish to visit **Pershore** town centre, it is suggested that, starting from
Drakes Broughton Church, you go right at the junction and, in 50 yards, take a
signposted path, left, around the edge of the recreation ground to go through a
gap in the hedge at the rear of a garage. Bear left on a narrow enclosed path to a
lane. On the lane, turn → and after ½ mile, having passed two farms, look out for
a footpath sign next to a gate on the left. Enter the field and go ↗ to a gap in the
hedge at the end. Pass through and turn sharp ←, following the field edge to the
far side, where you go through a gate in the fence. Descend ↗ to "Gig Bridge"
over Bow Brook. Cross this and go through a gate. Then go straight ahead along
a clear track through fields (Gig Bridge Lane) and onto a road by houses.
Descend to the main road (Station Road) in Pershore. Turn → *(the station is
about 1 mile left, on the right hand side of the road, just past the Coventry Arms
public house)*, then ← at the traffic lights and the town centre is straight on.

Quoting from the Tourist Information leaflet, "Famous for its elegant Georgian
architecture and important as the centre of a district rich in fruit and vegetable
production, Pershore has been designated a town of major architectural
importance by the Council of British Archaeology, and listed as an outstanding
conservation area." Note the imposing buildings with their arched coach
entrances in High Street, Bridge Street and Broad Street. Then, of course, there
is the magnificent Norman Abbey - or what remains of it. There is an indoor
market each Wednesday, Friday and Saturday. The River Avon fringes the town
at the opposite end from the station. Tourist Information is available from
Wanderers World Travel in High Street.

There is a bus service back to the station at certain times of the day. The bus
also serves Pinvin. If walking, it is about 1½ miles, so allow plenty of time. If you
prefer not to walk along the main road, you can take the turning before Station
Road on the right of High Street as you leave the town. Continue along Cherry
Orchard. Beyond a school, take a path on the right between the houses. Turn
← along the top of a grassy bank, alongside houses, emerging onto Mill Lane.
Here, a stile admits to a field. Cross and turn ↖ to a stile at the far end. Turn →
on the road and, opposite to the entrance to Wychavon Building Supplies, go
through a hedge gap on your left, by a signpost. Go along a path past a playing
field and alongside a hedge into Pershore Industrial Estate. Cross a driveway
and continue over rough ground by a hedge, up concrete steps to another drive.
Turn ← on the drive, then, straight away → and follow this as it bends left past
Kelly's Cafe to leave the trading estate on the driveway to Pershore station.

Walk 5 - Worcester to Pershore.

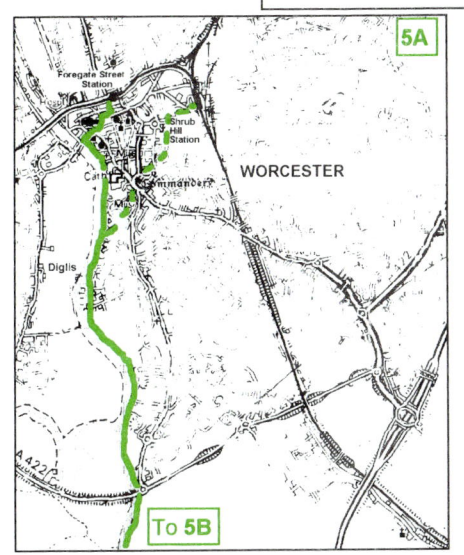

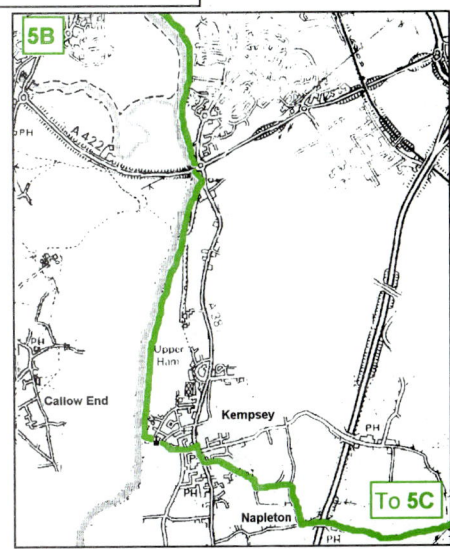

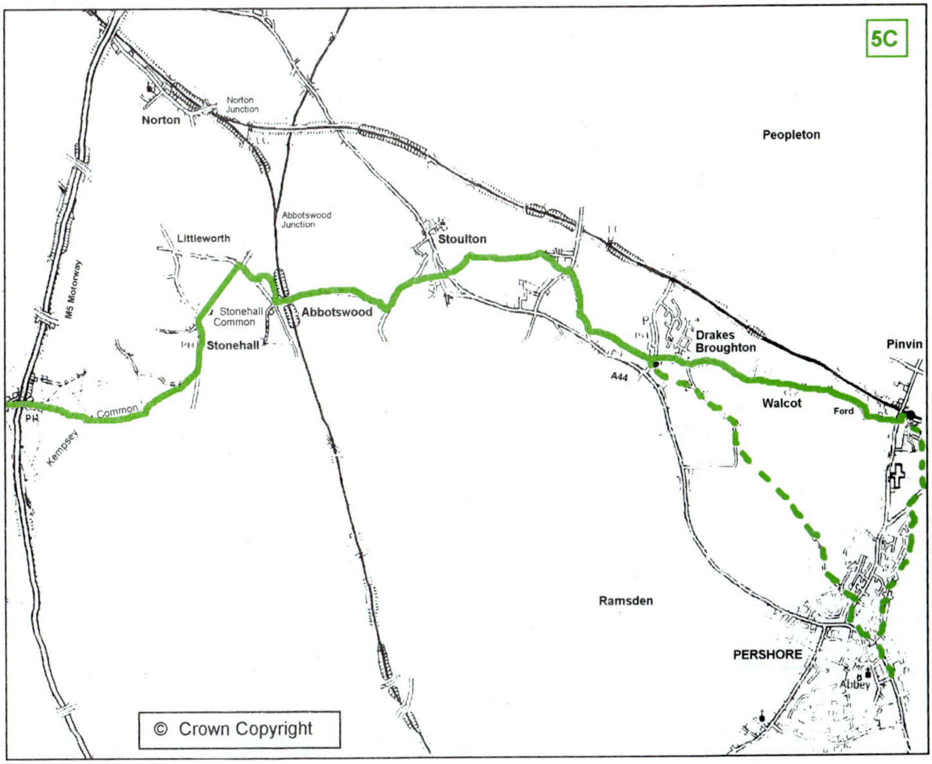

5A

Foregate Street Station
Shrub Hill Station
WORCESTER
Cathedral
Commandery
Mills
Diglis
A 422
To 5B

5B
PH
A 422
Upper Ham
Callow End
Kempsey
Napleton
PH
To 5C

5C
Norton Junction
Norton
Peopleton
Abbotswood Junction
Littleworth
Stoulton
M5 Motorway
Stonehall Common
Abbotswood
PH Stonehall
Drakes Broughton
Pinvin
A44
Walcot
Ford
Common
PH
Kempsey
Ramsden
PERSHORE
Abbey

© Crown Copyright

29

Above: About 2 miles from the start of the series of walks, we join the Wye Valley Walks. Here, looking back towards Hereford on **Walk number 1**, we see the River Wye, just beyond one of a series of kissing gates which were newly-installed in 1994.

Below: **Walk number 4** enters the city of Worcester via a footpath alongside the River Severn. A fine view can be obtained of the Cathedral, across the river. If you start from Foregate Street station, **Walk number 5** leaves the city along the footpath which can be seen on the opposite side of the river.

Above: A Cotswold town not on the normal tourist trail is Charlbury. This view from the town centre shows Church Street, at the bottom of which passes **Walk number 11.** A short detour will allow you take in the quiet air of the town, which contains many interesting old buildings.

Below: Nearing the end of the series of walks, a mile or so from the city of Oxford is this view of the River Thames, looking north. **Walk number 12** is on the left side of the photograph. In the distance, can be seen Wolvercote and on the right, Port Meadow.

6 PERSHORE to EVESHAM

8.7 miles
4 hours
14.0 kms.

Ordnance Survey 1:50000 series map 150.

The trouble with Pershore is that it is so far from its station, or should that be the other way around?   A brief description of the town is given at the end of Walk number 5. We did look at a possible walk which would include a visit to Pershore town centre but decided against it as, ultimately, it resulted in an extra 4½ miles to the route. We opted, instead, for a more direct, northern route which regretably involves more road walking than usual.   We start from Pershore station.

This is not a difficult walk but, as with all walks which are near to rivers, it can be muddy in parts and some places may be under water.

0.0   0.0   From the railway station, turn left half way along the driveway into the
(951480)   Industrial Estate. Go to the far end, past Kelly's Cafe *(open Mondays to Saturdays)* and bear right by a hedge, then cross a stile at a low yellow and black barrier on left into a field.   Go ↑ from stile and around hedge line, close to the railway line, passing the end of some earthworks. When reaching a road bridge, take a narrow path to the left, climbing to a stile and onto the B4084. Turn → through the village of **Wyre Piddle**, past the Anchor Inn *(bar meals)*.

0.9   0.9   On the outskirts of the village, before the road re-crosses the railway,
(968473)   follow a footpath sign → (to Lower Moor) to pass through a small white gate to the left of the house name sign "The Nait". An enclosed path between the houses emerges onto a driveway. Go over a stile then keep to the left of a black water tank to go forward along a slightly elevated dirt track.   After this bears right, take a narrow path, left, through the trees. Go over a small footbridge and across a field to some glasshouses at Lower End Farm.

1.1   2.0   Bear right, then left, to go right past and behind the farm buildings, then
(976469)   turn ←, taking a lane into **Lower Moor** village.   Turn → on footpath signposted to Blacksmith's Lane, around field edge, bearing left when you reach a track then turn right on Blacksmith's Lane to a T junction. Go ↑ here on a tarmac path across a field, gradually approaching the railway line. Go alongside it, then up some steps at the site of the former **Fladbury** station onto Station Lane.

1.3   3.3   Turn → on Station Lane, cross railway and go through the village,
(994467)   passing the Post Office and village stores and the Anchor Inn *(food available)*. *In the parish church can be seen in the Lady Chapel, a beautiful 14th century glass panel depicting the Virgin and Child.* Continue right through the village, after which, the road bends sharp left and goes over Jubilee Bridge at the River Avon.

The Jubilee Bridge was built in 1935, to replace the original one erected in 1885 to commemorate the Golden Jubilee of Queen Victoria in 1887.   The Hereford and Worcester County Countryside Service have positioned three picnic tables alongside the bridge, overlooking the river.   This may, therefore, be a convenient place for a break.

1.0   4.3   Having crossed the river, turn → and ascend to the village of
(001456)   **Cropthorne**.   Note the attractive church on your right.   Continue
ahead, passing the post office and the village school. *On the right is
Holland House, an attractive part-thatched black and white property,
originally three cottages, which was donated to the Church of England
Diocese of Worcester, by its owner, Mrs Ellis Holland and is now a
retreat house. It is not generally open to the public, but the gardens
can occasionally be visited as part of the National Gardens Scheme
(Photo on page 23).*   Turn ←, almost opposite, along Middle Lane,
and turn ← at T junction at the end.   Just round a right hand bend
follow a footpath sign to the right, straight across a field. Pass to the
right of a waymarked post then turn → at end of field. Go over a stile
near to the next corner then go ↖ across next field aiming for a
waymarked post in the opposite corner. Follow this to the left of a
fenced pond then go over a stile in the corner.   Follow the right hand
hedge to the end and go over 2 stiles and 2 footbridges on the right.
Keep to the left hand edge of the next three fields (stiles in between
them). Go over yet another stile in the corner and along the edge of a
thicket. Go over another stile and cross next field, again keeping to the
left side. A stile takes you onto a road.

1.9   6.2   Continue ↑ on a track through a field. At a former gateway, follow a
(014441)   yellow waymarker, turning → with a hedge on your right.   Part way
along the field boundary, a waymarker post indicates a ↖ turn to cross
the field, aiming slightly to the left of an electricity pylon to a stile and
footbridge in the hedge.   Cross and then go ahead, climbing through a
field, following power cables.   At the top of the field, go through a
metal gate to the right, then, immediately, left through a wicket gate to
enter a paddock. Pass through to exit by a stile into an old orchard.
Maintain the same heading with a hedge on your right to come out on a
rough-surfaced road.   Turn → and, just before the first house on the
left, follow a footpath to the left until you reach a kissing gate.

1.0   7.2   **At this point, you need to take a decision.** If the steeply descending
(027436)   field ahead is walkable (it was not when we researched it in February
1995, having been badly churned up by horses) you may like to go
through the kissing gate and descend to a stile at the bottom.   You
then pass under an access road to emerge at Hampton Ferry. You may
cross the river here, then proceed along the lane opposite, straight into
Evesham town centre.   The railway station is on left at other end of
High Street.   It is just short of a mile from the ferry to the station by this
route. *The ferry charge in 1994 was 30p for adults and 15p for
children. It operates from April to October only.* If you are unlucky and
find the ferry is not operating, turn → at the landing stage and go along
the river bank until the confluence with the River Isbourne is reached.
Bear to the right and onto the A44 road at ⊙ below. Returning to the
kissing gate, the walk, not using the ferry, continues by turning → along
a pathway which shortly becomes a road. This eventually joins the A44

road. Turn ← and in 0.2 mile ☉ you cross the River Isbourne. Go ahead to the traffic lights at the next crossroads where you turn ←.

0.8   8.0   Go over the River Avon bridge. Cross the road and descend the
(034431)   steps to follow an attractive river bank path through the Abbey Park. Follow this until near the next bridge. The path then bears slightly left. You can follow this up to Bridge Street where you turn ← through the main shopping area. Alternatively, you can turn ← to walk up the slope to go between the remains of the Benedictine Abbey. Once through, bear right, cross Market Place and you will be at the top of Bridge Street. Turn → into High Street. The walk ends
1.1   9.1   at the station which is about 700 yards on the left (037445).

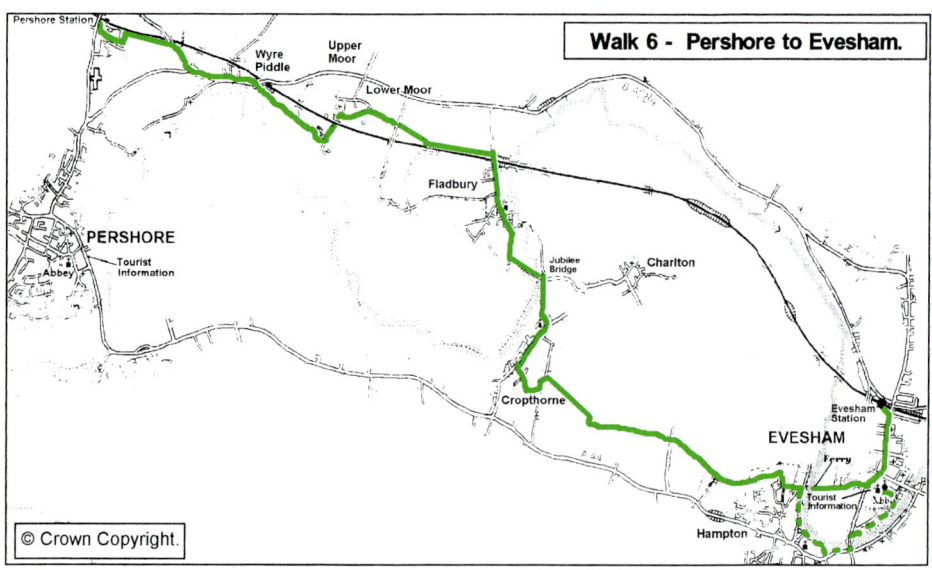

Walk 6 - Pershore to Evesham.

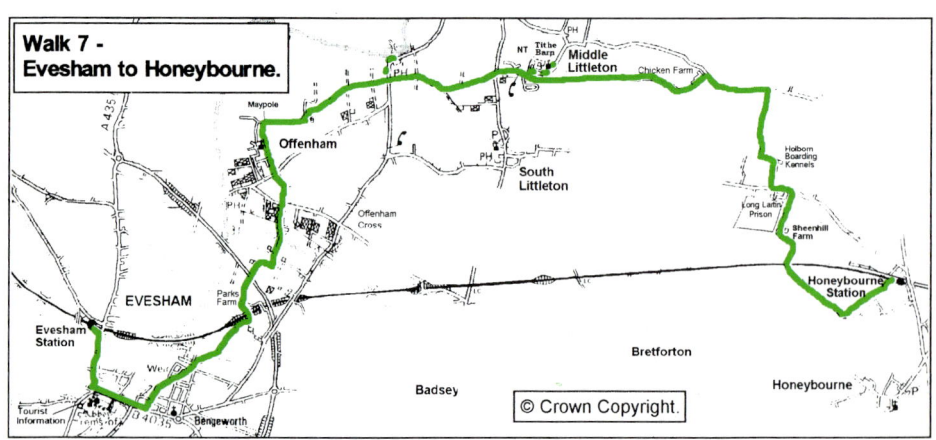

Walk 7 - Evesham to Honeybourne.

7 EVESHAM to HONEYBOURNE

Ordnance Survey 1:50000 series map 150.

8.5 miles
4 hours
13.7 kms.

Evesham is a busy market town sitting astride the River Avon. This walk takes you through the main shopping area, so there are plenty of places to obtain refreshments before you set out.   There are public toilets adjacent to the river bridge (on your right).   If you have time, you may like to look into the Almonry Museum, a 14th century building also used as the Tourist Information Centre.

This is not a particularly difficult walk, but if you decide to take any of the suggested detours, please allow extra time.

0.0   0.0   Starting from Evesham station, bear right at the end of the driveway
(037445)   into High Street. Follow this to the centre of the town where you can either turn left into Bridge Street, or you can walk down through the Abbey Park by crossing Market Place - market day, Saturday - *(note the 15th century half-timbered Booth Hall pictured on page 23)* and going along a passageway in the left hand corner which leads to the remains of the Benedictine Abbey.   Go through the bell tower, then descend to the bottom where a path leads, left, back to Bridge Street.

0.5   0.5   Cross the bridge over the River Avon, then, go straight ahead along
(039437)   Port Street, turning, ← at the Bear P.H. (Burford Road). Turn ←, along a footpath (Philipscote). At road, go ↗, on a track across a field. Take the first left fork, then go over a footbridge at a stream. Go forward to the end of an old orchard (either side of hedge).   Bear right along the top of the railway cutting then cross the line ←, by means of a bridge. *From here, there is a view of the tower of Evesham Abbey and Bredon Hill on the horizon.* Go ahead past Parks Farm House and downhill to cross the Evesham by-pass by ladder stiles on either side.   The track soon ends by a hedge at an old hut. Go →, along track, then follow round to the left, taking a left fork shortly afterwards. Go over a footbridge then pass a row of glasshouses. You will shortly arrive at a road junction in the village of **Offenham**.

2.0   2.5   Go straight ahead along Main Street, past the village stores and a
(055457)   cross roads and past the village church. At the end, by the tall red, white and blue maypole *(erected in September 1987)* turn →, along Gibbs Lane. This soon merges into a track, ending by a shed. Here, go ←, in front of the shed (waymarkers on it) to cross fields (slightly to the left) by a series of three stiles. Turn →, then, ←, and, ←, around field. At a corrugated shed turn →, into a field, keeping the hedge close to your right. The hedge bends to the left, then suddenly ends. Here, turn →, and cross the next field to a metal roadside gate.

1.2   3.7   Pass through gate, looking out for a footpath sign almost opposite. *An
(065469)   opportunity for refreshments exists here by going left along the road for around 100 yards to the Fish and Anchor public house by the banks of the River Avon, afterwards returning to the same spot.* The signpost points through a gateway and along a track which, crossing a field, rises through a wooded hollow to the top of Cleeve Hill. On the ridge

top, turn ←, along the track, descending to the village of **Middle Littleton**. At the road junction, go ↑, along School Lane.

1.0 4.7 When this bends sharply left, look out for a footpath sign opposite,
(078469) pointing through a gate into a paddock.

Before taking this route, a very worthwhile short diversion may be made to see the real gems of the village. Around the bend at a corner, where the road bends again to the right, can be seen over a low wall and across a meadow, the medieval tithe barn, manor house and parish church. The tithe barn, around 140 feet long by 40 feet wide, was constructed of beautiful blue lias with a dressing of Cotswold stone, sometime between 1286 and 1316 for the, then, Abbot of Evesham. It is the largest in the country and, arguably, is one of the finest, having recently been restored by the National Trust. Open daily, April to October, 9 to 5, admission 60p in 1994. ☎ (01684) 850051. In the grounds, there is also an impressive dovecote with around 750 holes. The manor house next door, also beautifully stone built, is of Elizabethan origin. The church alongside contains a Norman font.

Returning to the gate, go through, cross the paddock then go ↖, and over a stile. Go through next gate. This is the start of a long field path, through three fields by gates to a stile at the far side of a field. Cross, ↑, and, gradually coming nearer to the left hand field edge, head towards the far corner. Go over a stile, adjacent to a water tank, and cross the next field also keeping close to the hedge on your left. Go over a stile at the end and left through a gap in the hedge and, keeping the hedge close to your right, head for the field corner, where you cross a stile next to a gate into a small yard containing several chicken houses. Go between stream and first chicken house - go round the other side if you cannot get through - then, after keeping close to the stream on the right, go over a stile into a lane. Turn right in lane and, after ½ mile, at a footpath sign next to a red and white post, turn right on a track ending in the grounds of Holborn Boarding Kennels. Amidst the cacophony of barking dogs, turn right in front of the house along the driveway to the road opposite Long Lartin Prison.

2.3 7.0 Turn ←, along the road. When level with the rear of the last house, go
(102458) along a driveway on the right to Sheenhill Farm. Go ↑, between the farm buildings, Turn ← along farm track, then → at junction of tracks. Cross the railway line (remembering to close the gates at both sides). The path continues opposite, bearing ↖, then ↗ again ending in a long field. Bear ↖ across field and go through gate. Keep close to a hedge and stream on your right. Ignore a footbridge and stile in the far corner and continue around the field boundary. At the far end of next field, go into a caravan park through a gap in the hedge. Keep on the same general heading and go over a stile at the far side. This brings you to some former railway land. Bear → here and, in 100 yards, you
1.5 8.5 will arrive at the end of the walk at Honeybourne station (115448).

8 HONEYBOURNE to MORETON-IN-MARSH

Ordnance Survey 1:50000 series maps 150 and 151.

11.5 miles
6 hours
18.5 kms.

Honeybourne was once an important place on the railway network. It was the junction where the line from Birmingham Snow Hill and Stratford-upon-Avon to Cheltenham crossed the Oxford - Worcester route. When the former line closed in 1969, it was not considered that the small village nearby would generate sufficient traffic to warrant the retention of its station, so Honeybourne had to manage without a train service until 1981. In fact, it is still a junction - just. The line which turns away near to the station serves a spoil tip for Railtrack and ballast trains visit it on most weekdays. The remnant of the line to Stratford-upon-Avon is currently "mothballed" as it may be needed in the future, if the Army at Long Marston decide to use rail transport again. There is also a campaign to reinstate the line through to Birmingham but this is fraught with difficulties, mainly concerning road developments in the Stratford area. Honeybourne itself is a pleasant little village, through which you will pass on the walk.

Despite the fact that this walk starts in the flat lands of the Vale of Evesham, it does involve several strenuous climbs. It is not recommended for those in doubtful health. Some may prefer to walk it in the opposite direction as the climbs are not so severe and, as Honeybourne is some 250 feet lower than Moreton-in-Marsh, generally, you will be going downhill. Furthermore, the views tend to be more spectacular if you look at them from east to west.

0.0   0.0   From Honeybourne station, go along the driveway, then in the same
(115448) direction on Station Road *(past the Domestic Fowl Trust - Opening hours: 10.30 to 17.00 except Fridays)* to a crossroads by the Gate Inn. Bear right on High Street into Honeybourne, past the post office and "Thatched Tavern" public house. Bear left towards a church tower. Beyond the church (now a private dwelling) the lane ends in front of a metal gate. Enter the recreation ground here, cross and, keeping the hedge on your left go over (or around) the first stile, then, turn ➜ before the next stile in the hedge at the field corner and go to the road at the far end.

1.1   1.1   Turn ➜ on road, in 100 yards take a stile, left, at the entrance to
(117434) Weston Field farm. Go along the driveway and, when level with the house, go over a waymarked stile, right, then over a series of stiles through fields into the grounds of Long Stretch Farm. Turn ➜ over the bridge then ⬅ into a field with a stream on your left, through fields until a left-hand stile takes you over the track-bed of the former Stratford to Cheltenham railway line. Pass through a wicket gate into a field, crossing two stiles, always with the stream on your left. Look for a small stile and footbridge over the stream. Cross it and bear ➚ to a track in the centre of the field, aiming for a pole carrying power cables. Go through two gates, then ⬆ to the road at **Weston Sub Edge**.

1.3   2.4   Turn ➜ on the B4632 through the village, passing the Seagrave Arms
(126413) *(bar meals available)* and the Post Office-cum-village stores. There are several fine 17th century cottages along here. At a left bend is a

Above: **Walk number 8** is one of the more picturesque in our series - and one of the more strenuous. There are several fine panoramic views, especially looking towards the west. This one was taken during a short breather at a wayside bench above Broad Campden, with Chipping Campden in the distance.

Below: **Walks numbers 8 and 9** include the High Street (Fosse Way) in Moreton-in-Marsh. This view was taken in March 1991, before a mini roundabout was placed at the junction with the A44 road to Oxford. The large building on the left is the Redesdale Hall, named after Lord Redesdale (of Batsford), who had it built in 1887.

handy roadside bench to rest weary feet in preparation for the 530 foot climb yet to come. In around 400 yards past the bend, the road turns right. Bear left, then go ↑ along a road signed as *No Through Road*. This bends left, until, in front of a pair of garages, take a footpath to the right between houses. Go along field hedge, over footbridge and through kissing gate, then ↗, to the far corner of the next field. There is a fine view of the parish church to your left. Cross two stiles, bear right then go through the left hand of a pair of field gates, crossing two fields with the hedge and stream close to you on your left. In the far left corner of the second field, do not go through the gate ahead but turn ←, cross a footbridge by two stiles and go along a right-hand field boundary, following waymarkers. At the field corner, in front of two stiles with footbridges, keeping in the same field, turn sharp ← and ascend slope to the left of a house, aiming for a footpath sign, clearly seen. Continue climbing steeply and cross a stile in the hedge on the sky line. Cross the centre of the next field, going over a stile in the middle, to the top hedge line. From here, in clear weather, there is a glorious view behind you of Bredon Hill, the Malverns ridge and the Vale of Evesham. Turn ← with the hedge close to your right and cross a stile to a road. Turn right and climb for 150 yards to a kissing gate at a National Trust sign on the left. Pass through then turn ↗ and climb through a shallow gully to the 754 foot summit of Dovers Hill.

1.8   4.2   There are several benches hereabouts and a topograph. To continue,
(137396)   walk along the ridge top away from the car park. You are now on the "Cotswold Way", which starts in Bath and runs to Chipping Campden. Just beyond the trig pillar, locate a waymarked stile in the hedge on your right. Go over and along a field boundary to Kingcomb Lane. Turn ← here and, in 50 yards, turn →, downhill, to follow "Cotswold Way" signs on a footpath opening onto a track then a road into Chipping Campden. Turn ← at the T Junction into High Street.

1.3   5.5   **Chipping Campden** is a fine Cotswold town. It has a range of shops,
(151391)   cafes, public houses etc. There are public toilets in Sheep Street (next turning on right off High Street). The Tourist Information Office is in High Street. The town did have a railway station but this closed in 1966, although there is talk of a possible reopening. To continue the walk, turn →, opposite Town Hall, through an archway next to the Post Office. Much of the route from here follows the "Heart of England Way" and is waymarked. After passing a cafe and car park, go ↑ along George Lane. Continue ↑ where the road narrows.

0.4   5.9   A road joins from the right. Join this and continue straight on.
(153385)   (Alternatively, a path appears to run just behind the hedge on your left if you prefer to use it). After about 350 yards, where the road bends right, a path forks to the left. Take this and, in 200 yards, go ↑ across a field where the track appears to bear right. Go through a gap in the hedge opposite then bear ↗ across next field, where, through a gap in

the bottom corner, you cross a stream and a stile. Join another path and bear to the right under the trees. Ignore a turn to the left and go ↑ through a gate. When you reach a road, turn left and shortly, at main road, turn →. You are now in the picturesque village of **Broad Campden**. This is well worth a short detour if you have time to wander around.

0.8   6.7   Ignore the road to the left and, shortly (opposite a house named "Izods
(158378)   Close"), take a footpath, left, upwards over a stile. Go straight across the steeply rising field, aiming for a stile in the left hedge towards the top. Cross stile into a lane. There is a handily placed bench almost opposite to get your breath back and to admire the view of Chipping Campden *(see photo on page 38)*. Enter a spinney (opposite the previous stile) and turn → to walk through the trees just a few yards from the road. At the end of spinney, go over stile and turn → back to the road.

0.6   7.3   Turn ← and follow the road for about half a mile. At a sharp left hand
(161368)   bend, a path climbs, right, up the bank. Take this and go through a gate on the left and, shortly, through a second gate. Head slightly to the right down the field and through a gateway at the bottom. Climb steeply up the next field, heading ↗. Go between the Horse Chestnut trees at the top of the hill, then keep on the same heading. You will come to a stile a few yards from the right hand end of a wire mesh fence. Go through, then follow a path, ↗, across a field. Go over a stile next to a house, then down the path to a road. Go ↑, then turn ← at a grassed area known as "Back Ends" down Bell Bank. This brings you into **Blockley** - yet another picturesque Cotswold village which is well worth a little exploration before proceeding.

0.8   8.1   Turn →, just before the church. Turn ←, just past the Old Bakery and
(163348)   before the Old Crown Inn and Hotel. At the bottom, follow the road round to the left. You will shortly reach a main road, where you turn ← and look for a footpath sign on the right about 150 yards away. Follow this (signed "The Duck Paddle"), then go over a stile next to a gate. Go over the next stile then follow a waymark on a pole ↗ across the steeply rising field. Aim to the right of Park Farm, which, incidentally, was advertising Bed and Breakfast at the time of the survey in October 1994. There is a stile in a corner which juts into the field. Go over this then go ↖, still upwards, gradually getting nearer to the left-hand hedge. For an excuse to catch your breath, take time look back at the glorious view over Blockley.

0.8   8.9   At a gate, turn ← among some trees. When you reach another gate,
(169341)   go through, then immediately → through a second (smaller) gate. Keep to the right hand side of the next two fields then emerge onto a road through some trees. Cross this road, then keep ↑ following the stone wall of Batsford Park on your left and, in the main, woods on your right. After crossing another track, the path starts to descend steeply.

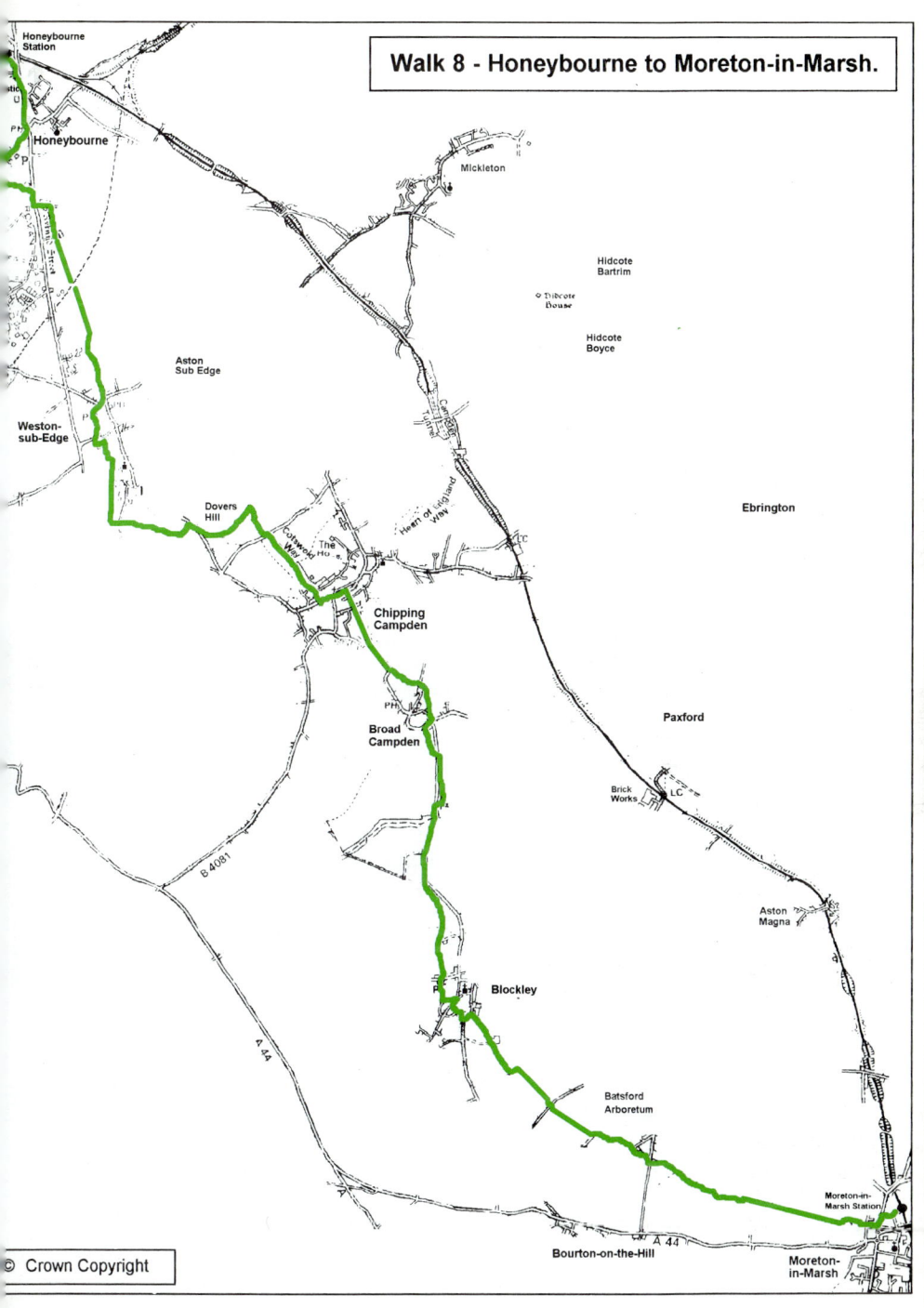

Walk 8 - Honeybourne to Moreton-in-Marsh.

Honeybourne Station

Honeybourne

Mickleton

Hidcote
Bartrim

Hidcote
House

Hidcote
Boyce

Aston
Sub Edge

Weston-
sub-Edge

Ebrington

Dovers
Hill

The
House

Chipping
Campden

Paxford

Broad
Campden

Brick
Works

Aston
Magna

B 4081

Blockley

A 44

Batsford
Arboretum

Moreton-in-
Marsh Station

Bourton-on-the-Hill

Moreton-
in-Marsh

When you reach a gateway on the left, turn ➔, then, shortly, ← along next track. When you see a lodge on your left look for a stile in the fence opposite, slightly to your right. Go over stile then head ↑ across field, heading for another lodge. Go through gate, where you cross the main driveway to Batsford Arboretum and go through a kissing gate to the right of the house.

0.9	9.8	Cross the next field, aiming for the far left hand corner. Ignore a
(183331)		convergence of tracks on the left and go through another kissing gate

0.9   9.8   Cross the next field, aiming for the far left hand corner. Ignore a
(183331) convergence of tracks on the left and go through another kissing gate at the end. Keep to the left of the next two fields, separated by kissing gate, going over a stone footbridge towards the end of the second field. Go through a kissing gate then head for two large trees. Go through kissing gate in far hedge then ↑ across next four fields, the last having a kissing gate in a sharply slanting hedge on the left. Go through, then turn ➔, keeping a large oak tree on your right. You will come to a kissing gate. Go through, alongside allotments, to emerge into Hospital Road. Go straight on along Corders Lane (not named at this end) to emerge into **Moreton-in-Marsh** High Street near to the Redesdale Hall *(see photo on page 38)*. Cross the main road (The Fosse Way) and turn ←. You can reach the railway station by turning ➔ down New Road, then turning ↖ into the driveway. This is the end

1.7   11.5   of the walk.   Grid ref 207327.

Below: A scene which is typical of the north Cotswolds and of walks in that area. It portrays a ewe and lambs in a field at Bledington on the Gloucestershire/Oxfordshire border. In the distance can be seen Bledington church. If you cannot find this view, do not worry. We are cheating a little as it was taken from just the other side of the village to the route of **Walk number 9**.
Photo: Tim Shirley.

9 MORETON-IN-MARSH to KINGHAM

Ordnance Survey 1:50000 series maps 151 and 163.

11.0 miles
5 hours
17.7 kms.

Moreton-in-Marsh is a place which is used as a stopping-off point on a long journey. It always was thus, being a staging point on the ancient Fosse Way. Therefore it bustles, especially on a Tuesday (market day). High Street is wide and lined with Cotswold stone buildings. There are numerous small shops and several cafes, some of which may not appreciate the sight of walking-boots! Our walk starts at Moreton station which is near the town centre.

Although slightly longer than the average walk, the route for this one is not strenuous. There are hills, but not steep ones. Allow a little extra time to wander around the Cotswold villages you will encounter.

0.0 0.0 Walk up from Moreton-in-Marsh station, turn right along New Road
(207327) (past Post Office) and then left into the High Street. There are toilets in front of the Redesdale Hall and in Corders Lane. Continue along High Street, passing the Manor House Hotel.

0.4 0.4 Turn ➔ along Parkers Lane, passing the Fire and Ambulance Stations
(204321) on your left. At gate, turn ⬅, following footpath sign "Sezincote Longborough". Continue straight on at end of metalled access road. Go through metal gate into a field then keep following right hand hedge. Go over stile into next field and again follow right hand hedge. You will then emerge part way along another field. Turn ➔ and, once again, follow right hand hedge. Straight on through gate (yellow waymarker). Go over a stile and through a gate then bear slightly to the left, aiming for a metal gate to right of a tree. Go through gate, keep to left of next field then go through another gate. Go straight on to a point about half way across next field, then turn right. Go through gap in the hedge, then follow line of power cables to corner of wood. Go through gate to your left then follow tractor tracks round to the right. At end of field, go through gate and past a dutch barn.

1.5 1.9 Straight on at next gate (it has two waymarks on it) and, in a few yards,
(185310) join the farm driveway. Keep following this (left and right bends) through three gates. It is suggested that you look back at the view behind you when nearing the top of the last field.

0.7 2.6 At cattle grid turn ⬅ following top edge of the field. You may like to
(175307) make a short detour before your left turn. If you go through a kissing gate on your right, you will emerge into a field from where, about 200 yards further on, you will have an excellent view of **Sezincote House** on your left. This imposing oriental looking building was erected by Sir Charles Cockerell early in 19th century and is said to have provided the inspiration for the Brighton Pavilion. Return to the cattle grid, mentioned above, then after following top edge of the field go through another gate and now keep the fence on your left. Keep on towards the church ahead which is in the village of **Longborough**.

0.7 3.3 When you reach the village turn ⬅ down the road and then take the

(178297) right-hand road towards Stow-on-the-Wold. Take the next road on the left which has a "No Through Road" sign. Continue straight on at the end of the tarmac and at the next gate keep left on the track to **Donnington**. Where the obvious track veers left, keep straight on with the wire fence on your right and go through a gate into the wood. Go through the gate at the end of the wood and cross the field diagonally right to the gate at the top of the wooden fence. Keep to the left of the buildings ahead, go through two gates and keep close to the wall of Donnington Manor (there is no way-marking here). Pass through the gate, turn ← on to the road and keep left down the road.

1.6 4.9 At the main road (A429) go straight across and down the road to
(198280) **Broadwell** Church. At the road junction before the church take the road to Stow briefly and walk up the path into the churchyard. At the end of the churchyard path, cross the drive and keep close to the wall on your right. Go through the gate at the bottom end of the field and follow the road down into the village. Opposite the Fox Inn cross the village green and take the road to Oddington.

0.7 5.6 Ignore the road to Evenlode and go through the gate a short distance
(206274) on, on your right. Cross the open field and then keep the hedges immediately on your left until you cross a stream. Go over the stiles and up the field, making for the right-hand corner of the field with a small electricity pylon. Take the path to the left towards the farm buildings with the hedge on your right. Pass through the gate between the buildings, turn →, behind the house, and go over the stile. Walk across the field to the gap in the hedge (waymark) and follow the wide path. Turn ←, down to the farm and then →, on to the main (A436) road. Cross road, turn → and go down the hill to **Upper Oddington**.

1.5 7.1 Bear left down to the village and turn ← again. Where the road bears
(221258) left go right down the "No Through Road" and, at the house at the end of the road, take the path alongside the right-hand wall of the house. Cross the field to the far right-hand corner, cross the stile and continue straight across the next field.

1.0 8.1 Turn → on to the road and continue on the track past the church.
(232257) Where the track enters a wood take the path to the right (blue waymark) and when it emerges into a field go ←. Keep going along the left-hand sides of a number of large fields, with the hedges immediately on your left. At the end of the last field go left through the gate and turn right on to a wide track. This track leads to the main road to the picturesque centre of **Bledington.** If, however, you wish to shorten the walk, go over a stile on left where track bends right. Cross field via bridge over stream in middle, aiming to the right of two power cable poles. Go over stile and follow path to ←. Turn ← on road at ¤.

1.7 9.8 Returning to the original route, turn ← on to main road and follow it
(242230) through the village, crossing stream and turning ← in centre. At the

Post Office, go ↑ (No Through Road) ⌘. At end of the lane, pass to right of a house then go over stile next to a gate. Turn ← and follow field round to the right. Keep ↑, passing footbridge over a stream on your left. Keep the stream on your left. Follow River Evenlode past the sewage works. Continue alongside the river over several stiles. Turn 1.2 11.0 ← at road.   Kingham Station (256227) is about 500 yards on left.

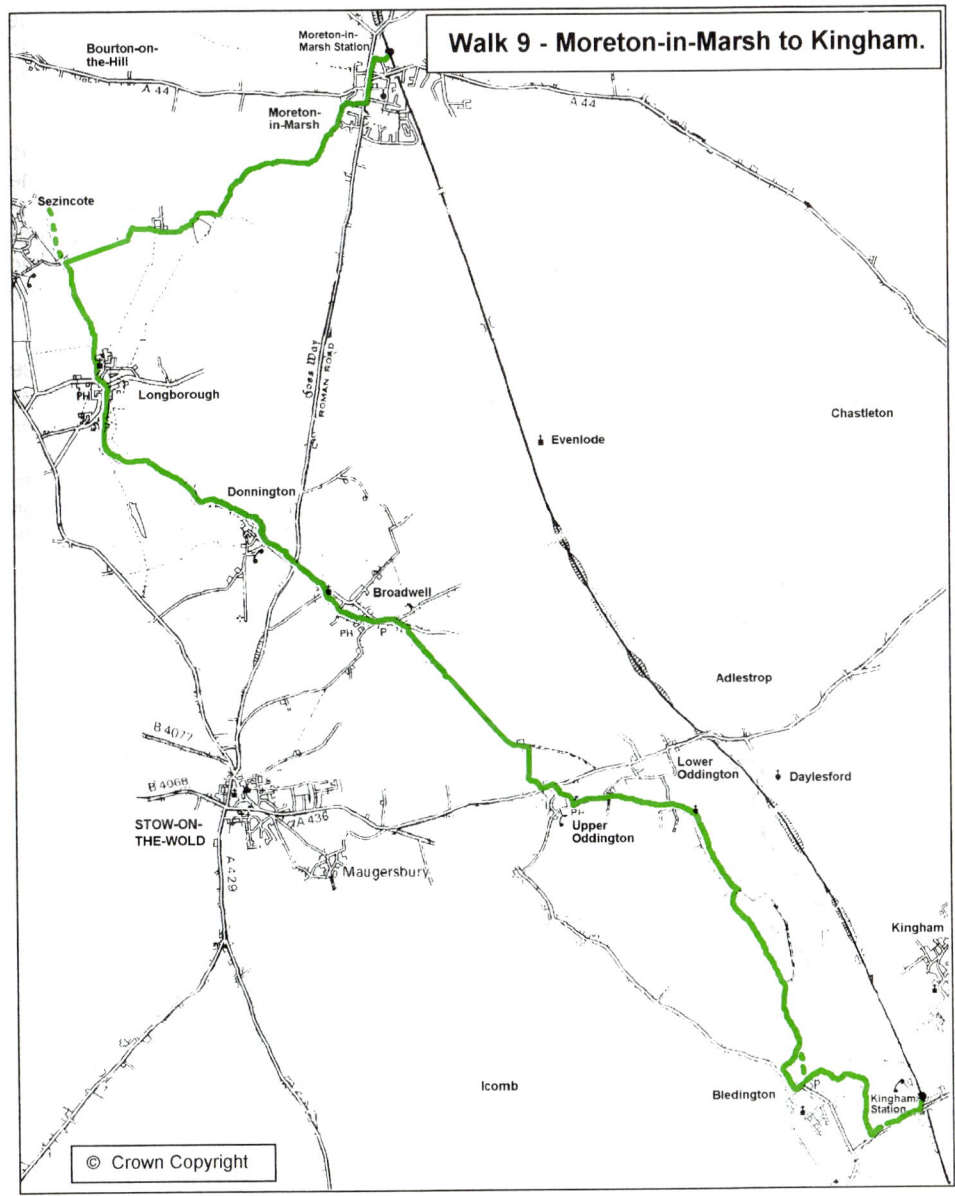

Walk 9 - Moreton-in-Marsh to Kingham.

Bourton-on-the-Hill

Moreton-in-Marsh Station

Moreton-in-Marsh

A 44

A 44

Sezincote

Longborough

FOSS WAY ROMAN ROAD

Evenlode

Chastleton

Donnington

Broadwell

PH   P

Adlestrop

B 4077

Lower Oddington

Daylesford

B 406B

STOW-ON-THE-WOLD

A 436

Upper Oddington

A 429

Maugersbury

Kingham

Icomb

Bledington

Kingham Station

Cross next field aiming for a point about 100 yards from right hand corner where another stream is crossed by a footbridge. Cross next field ↗ aiming for sign post on road at far right hand corner.

0.3   5.3   You now encounter a triangle in the road. Fork left, then go straight
(381147)   across to gateway at other end of triangle. Go through gate then keep to left side of hedge.   At bottom turn →.   After about 100 yards turn ← up steep hill through a small wood. Go ↑ across field, through gap in hedge, bear ↖ across next field then follow hedge to corner. Go over stile then follow hedge on your right until you reach a gap in it. Go through this gap then continue to follow hedge, keeping it on your left, until you reach a stile in it. Go over stile, then follow path straight on to village of East End. Nearby (396153) is **North Leigh Roman Villa** (turn left, then right).   A visit will add about a mile to your walk.

1.1   6.4   If continuing from where you joined the road through the village, turn →
(396148)   then look for "Footpath" sign on left pointing to pathway across a front lawn and between two houses. **East End** is a pleasant   little village and is the only place on the walk where refreshments may be obtained. The "Leather Bottel" public house advertises food and is situated two hundred yards further along on the right.   However, it is recommended that you return to this path to restart the walk as, if you take another turning you will miss out the quaintest part of the village.   Take the path between the houses, go over two stiles then turn →.

0.3   6.7   At "Nab Cottage" two tracks cross. Turn ← (yellow arrow). Pass "The
(400146)   Croft" then turn →. Where path bends to left, turn → along path which joins.   Turn ← at junction with next path and cross a small stream. Goo up hill and follow edge of wood until another track is met on left (laurel hedge on corner). Turn ← still keeping wood on left. At end of this wood, keep straight on, then keep Mill Wood on your right.   You will now see the Blenheim Saw Mill on your left, just across the River. Bear right just before a gate, and follow the fence around a new tree plantation. You will soon reach the River Evenlode. Keep straight on alongside river. You will then reach a metal stile and a road.

1.4   8.1   Turn ← along the road as far as the river bridge. **If you wish to catch**
(419147)   **a train from Combe Halt,** this is about 300 yards away - turn left after going under the bridge. Our walk continues by turning → just before the **river** bridge, following river for a hundred yards or so. At a gate, fork right (blue waymarker) and walk up opposite side of field to railway line. Near top of hill, the path passes through the hedge. Continue straight on, under large Horse Chestnut tree then join metalled lane.

0.6   8.7   At Main Road, turn ←.   You are now about three quarters of the way
(427143)   along the village of Long Hanborough, most of which (including the shops and public houses) is to your right.   The walk ends at Hanborough station which is on the right hand side, just over the
0.4   9.1   railway bridge (Grid Ref 433142).

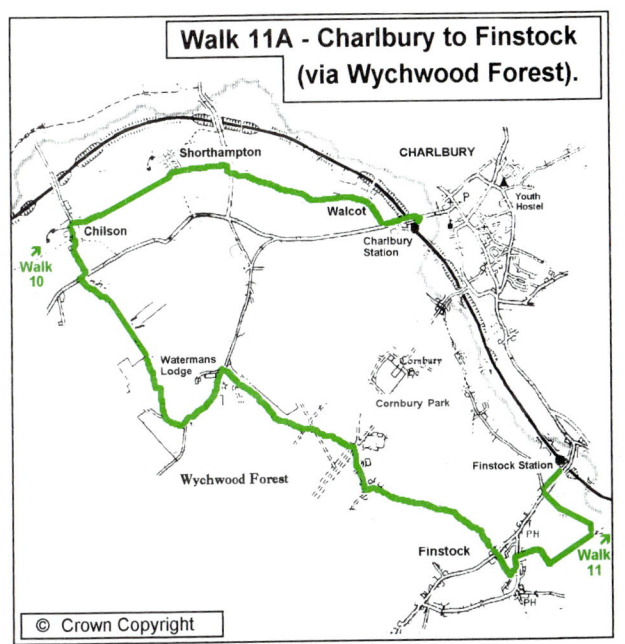

Walk 11A - Charlbury to Finstock (via Wychwood Forest).

Shorthampton

CHARLBURY

Walcot

Chilson

Charlbury Station

Walk 10

P

Youth Hostel

Watermans Lodge

Cornbury

Cornbury Park

Finstock Station

Wychwood Forest

Finstock

PH

Walk 11

© Crown Copyright

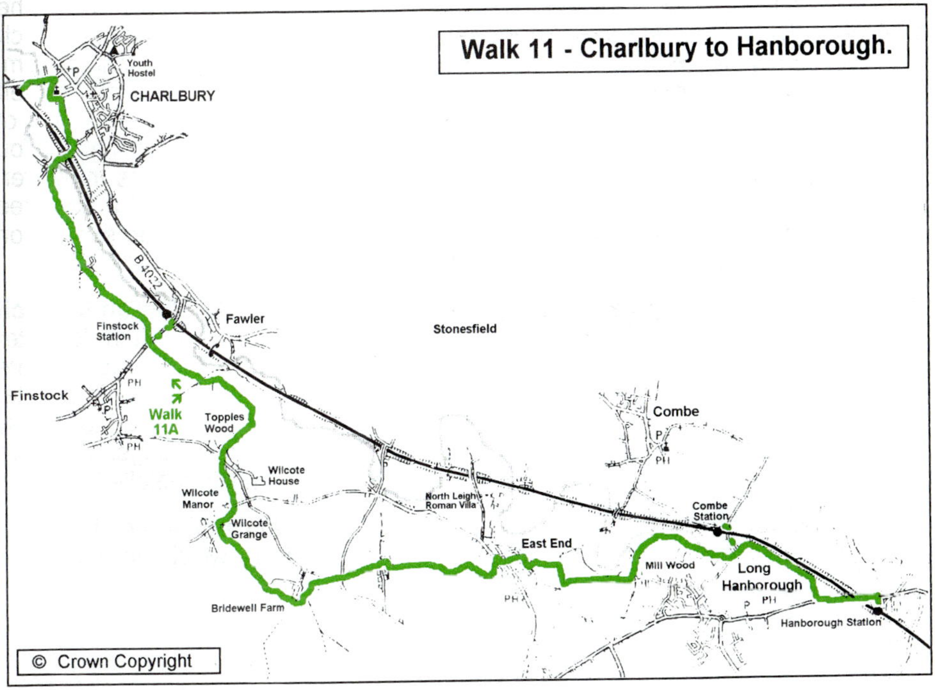

Walk 11 - Charlbury to Hanborough.

Youth Hostel

CHARLBURY

B 4022

Finstock Station

Fawler

Stonesfield

Finstock

PH

Walk 11A

Topples Wood

Combe

P

PH

Wilcote House

Wilcote Manor

North Leigh Roman Villa

Combe Station

Wilcote Grange

East End

Mill Wood

Long Hanborough

PH

Bridewell Farm

PH

Hanborough Station

© Crown Copyright

51

CHARLBURY to FINSTOCK

Ordnance Survey 1:50000 series map 164.

7.6 miles
3.5 hours
12.2 kms.

As an alternative to walk number 11, readers may like to try this half day ramble mainly using the route of the *Charlbury Circular Walk*. Until a few years ago, access to the Wychwood Forest was severely restricted. Then, Oxfordshire County Council decided that a path should be opened, straight through the middle of it and so, the Circular Walk was born. Our walk deviates from the Circular Walk route to arrive at a point nearer to Finstock station from where you may return by train, but, please check the times first as services are very restricted. The Cotswold Line Promotion Group has included this walk to encourage more use of Finstock station, which was in severe danger of closure in 1994.

With the exception of a few short steep parts, this walk is comparatively easy. There are a few places which are likely to be muddy, especially in the forest.

0.0   0.0   Leave Charlbury station and turn ← at the end of the driveway. Go
(352194)   over railway bridge then take first turn → at sign to "Walcot only" (also sign "Circular Walk Bridleway"). Follow lane. At two cottages on right, keep straight on signed "Bridleway to Chilson".

1.3   1.3   When you reach a road, turn → then ← towards Shorthampton. Where
(333200)   road bears right, keep ↑. Where lane bears right, again keep ↑ through green gate, ignoring footpath sign to the left. The track eventually emerges onto a road at Chilson.

1.0   2.3   Turn ←. *After about 200 yards, walk number 10 (from Kingham) joins*
(318196)   *from the right at post box.* Continue straight on until you reach a T junction.

0.3   2.6   Turn →, then, after about 100 yards, turn ← following "Circular Walk"
(320191)   sign (also signed "Chilson Hill only"). Keep straight on under tree and along a twisting grassy path, bearing right at a fork to emerge into a field. Follow left hand edge of field then go through gap in top corner. Follow edge of wood on left, passing a clearing in it.

0.6   3.2   Shortly, enter wood where it crosses the path (yellow arrow way-
(325184)   marker). Fork right following another yellow waymark. At end of firs, turn ← then →. On leaving wood, go along track (hedge on left) around field. The path emerges onto a lane.

0.5   3.7   Turn ← and follow lane for about 700 yards. On reaching "Watermans
(329176)   Lodge Stables", turn → over stile, signed "Circular Walk Finstock 2". Follow yellow arrow into wood, bearing right. At next fork, bear left (another yellow arrow). Path emerges into a wide grassy "ride" through the trees. Follow this gently downhill.

1.3   5.0   At bottom, there is a gate on the left leading to Cornbury House
(345175)   (private). Here, the path crosses another wide ride, known as "Grand Vista". Join a track which bears to the right and follow this past a

sawmill. The path now descends to a pool on the right. Here, follow path round to the left which goes steeply uphill. At fork, bear left. Go ↑ at cross tracks and over stile. You then emerge from the wood. Keep following track.

1.2 6.2 Track emerges onto a main road on the outskirts of the village of
(359165) **Finstock**. Go straight across, bearing slightly to the right. Keep straight on at end of church yard, then turn left at end of playing field and follow the path down to the road.

0.2 6.4 At road (School Road) turn ← then turn → down Wards Lane. *If you*
(361165) *require provisions, the Spa supermarket, just past Wards Lane, is open until 8.00pm each weekday and Saturday.* Just beyond the last house in Wards Lane, bear right (ignore disused stile). Descend steeply into valley. Cross stile at bottom and turn ← onto another footpath. In about 450 yards, look out for a path on the left where the main path bends to the right.

0.6 7.0 *At this point, you may join the Charlbury to Hanborough walk (number*
(368166) *11) by following this path to the right.* Our walk takes the path to the left. Almost immediately, there is a second turning to the left. Take this path, ignoring a stile on your right. Shortly, climb a bank to emerge in the corner of a field. *(There used to be a stile here).* On entering a field, bear left following about 10 yards from the edge. The path, here, is indistinct but becomes clearer when you reach the brow of the hill. Aim for a clump of trees in front of which is a pole carrying power cables. Join track which comes in from the left, then follow concrete driveway to main road. At main road, turn →, but be careful as traffic tends to travel at high speeds. Finstock station (366172) is 300 yards
0.6 7.6 on the left.

If you find that you are short of time to catch your train at Finstock station, you may turn left and walk straight down the main road from Grid Ref 359165, a distance of about 1000 yards. If you miss your train, there is a pleasant footpath through Cornbury Park, starting opposite to the point where the above walk joins the main road 300 yards from the station. This footpath will take you back to Charlbury. Turn left where you emerge in Park Street from Cornbury Park driveway. Turn left through church yard then go along Church Lane to its junction with Dyers Hill. Charlbury station is about 200 yards on the left.

Those wanting a longer day out may like to try a combination of Walks 10, 11 and 11A. This offers the possibility of walks from Kingham to Finstock (12.1 miles), Combe (17.2 miles) or Hanborough (18.0 miles) or Charlbury to Combe (12.6 miles) or Hanborough (13.4 miles), *via the Wychwood Forest*. Please remember that train services at Combe and Finstock are very restricted. Both stations were subject to a closure proposal in 1994 but were, thankfully, reprieved on a technicality. Thames Trains, who have since become responsible for these two stations are understood not to have any immediate plans for closure.

12 HANBOROUGH to OXFORD

Ordnance Survey 1:50000 series map 164.

10.6 miles
5 hours
17.1 kms

The village of Long Hanborough is what it says, "long". From the station, it stretches over a mile along the A4095 westwards towards Witney. In fact, much of the village is nearer to Combe station than to Hanborough! Our final walk in the series starts at Hanborough station, the main claim to fame for which was that it was the destination for Sir Winston Churchill's funeral train on 30th January 1965. Sir Winston is buried one mile away at Bladon church.

Do not attempt this walk during particularly wet weather as the River Thames overflows its banks and parts between Eynsham and Oxford can become impassable.

0.0   0.0   Leave the station by turning ← at the end of the driveway. For safety,
(433142)   you need to cross the busy main road, as the footpath is on the opposite side. Go over the railway bridge then up a slight incline. Almost at the top, there is a "Footpath" sign on left between "Elmwood", "Pinsley House and Pinsley Orchard" signs. Cross the road again and go along a short driveway. There is a narrow path alongside a small open space on your left. Follow this and go over stile into a field. Bear, ↖, across field aiming for a gate which has a stile alongside. Go over stile then follow the right hand edge of the next field. Go through gap in the hedge then past two dutch barns.

0.7   0.7   At a junction of tracks, turn →, and follow this until you reach a small
(433137)   gate in the hedge. Go through, then straight on, following edge of the field, alongside a wood. At the end of the field, the official path goes left to road, then back again ↖ across next field. Local practice seems to be to turn →, into the wood, then turn ← to follow a path just inside the wood boundary, until you reach a fork in the paths (near where the field outside the wood ends) - the official route joining from the left near here. Fork right. Shortly another path joins from the left. Follow this to the right, still keeping just inside the wood. This emerges into a field. Keep to left side of field until you meet a fence on the right. Follow this until you enter village of **Church Hanborough** opposite the church. The Church here is dedicated to St Peter and St Paul and is well worth a visit. The village itself is very pleasant with many Cotswold stone cottages, some thatched, and glorious flower displays in summer.

0.9   1.6   At Church Hanborough, turn ←, then take the lane, signposted
(426129)   "Freeland", to the right. The lane, which is very narrow and steep sided, descends steeply. Beware should you be unfortunate enough to meet a vehicle. At the bottom, turn ←, (signposted "Circular Walk Footpath Freeland 1"). There are two fields here, divided by a hedge. The path goes into the left hand field. Follow hedge on the right. At the top, turn ← as far as cable pole. The path turns → here, through a gate. Bear ↖, across the next small field and go through next gate. Turn →, and follow the hedge on your right. Go over stile at bottom corner then keep following hedge round to the right. Go over stile.

Again keep following the hedge, ignoring a stile in it. At the top of the field, go over the stile in the corner, by some houses. You are now at the end of the village called **Freeland**.

0.9 2.5 Turn ← along an unmetalled bridleway. In about 200 yards there is a
(417121) fork in the path. Take the left fork and follow trees on your right. Go through trees/bushes at end of field then again keep to right of next field. Same again in next field. Pass a gap in the hedge, then, about 25 yards from the bottom, look for a stile hidden in the thick high hedge on your right. Go over this and again follow right hand hedge. At bottom there is a stile and footbridge over stream.

0.8 3.3 Go over this then follow path to right into a field. Follow left hand
(421111) hedge until you reach a waymarker post, where you follow arrow, slightly to left into bushes. Cross another footbridge/stile then continue along left hand side of field and over another stile in left hand corner. You are now in a small field. The next stile is on your right when you reach the bottom left hand end of field. In fact there are two, separated by a timber crossing of a ditch. Cross these and enter field, then follow hedge on your right. Go over stile by a gate and continue along right side of next field. Go over yet another stile where path goes between hedges. There is a junction of paths here.

0.5 3.8 Ignore the one to your right. Within a few yards, continue ↑ along a
(425104) well used track between hedges. In about 500 yards you will reach the A40. trunk road. Immediately on your left is a Little Chef Café and, next to that, a garage where takeaway refreshments can be obtained.

0.3 4.1 At this point, **please take the utmost care.** The A40 is one of the
(429100) busiest and most dangerous roads in the country. There are NO official crossing places in this area, and you may have to wait a long time to cross. Be patient. Alternatively, you may prefer to walk 700 yards or so to the left to cross at a roundabout where there is a central refuge. You can then turn right and follow this road until you reach the second roundabout (i.e from the first one), where you rejoin the walk proper at point ●.

Reverting to the normal walk, having crossed the A40 road, go along a short footpath leading to a road in a residential area. Continue in the same direction along this until you reach a T junction. Turn → into Mill Street and follow this into the village, turning ← at the end.

Eynsham is a smart little place with public toilets (along path to your right, just before you reach the village centre) a range of shops and public houses and one, rather up-market, restaurant. It is a good place for a break.

0.6 4.7 Re-start the walk at St. Leonard's church. Proceed past the Red Lion
(432092) public house and follow the road (High Street) to the right. This soon becomes Oxford Road. Keep straight on until you reach a roundabout,

● which, incidentally, together with the road to the right, is on the track-bed of the old railway line from Yarnton to Fairford. Again, keep straight on (signposted Farmoor and Botley). Keep following roadside footpath as far as the Swinford Toll Bridge - *a road sign before it says 1 mile but means ¼!* Cross the River Thames by this bridge (no charge for pedestrians).

0.8   5.5   At end of the bridge, turn ← (Signposted "Oxford 5"), bearing right at a
(442089)   fork in the path.   Follow the river bank past Eynsham Lock.   Keep following the river bank path, eventually passing between the river and Wytham wood.

0.8   6.3   At the second kissing gate you reach, turn →, to follow a path which
(454092)   goes up to the wood, then follow the edge of it.   Turn →, when you reach a gate (waymarked).   When you reach the wood again, keep following the edge of it - DO NOT veer left where the main track does so.   At end of next field, turn ←, then in 50 yards turn →.   *You will probably note that the edges of the fields in this area are all marked out with sticks.   This is part of an Oxford University long term ecological experiment.   Please do not disturb the various types of vegetation growing there.*   Cross a track, go over a stile then go up the right hand side of field.   At top, go ↑, over another stile.   Again keep to right edge of the field.   You will now get your first glimpse in the distance ahead of the "Dreaming Spires" of Oxford.

1.0   7.3   Go through a gap in the hedge and turn ←.   Follow the track down the
(469091)   left side of the field.   Cross straight over a lane and proceed to a farm. Go through the farm then swing right going over bridge over stream. Go over stile.   Bear ↖, across the water meadows.   Go over two stiles in the corner, then aim for the large bridge which carries the Oxford by-pass (A34) over the River Thames.

0.8   8.1   Go through a gate and under the bridge. Keep following the river bank
(481093)   path. Cross road, then follow river, past the ruins of Godstow Nunnery. Then pass Godstow Lock. The famous Port Meadow pasture land now appears on the opposite bank of the river. Often, flocks of geese can be seen here, and cattle seem to like paddling in the river. Keep following the river bank path and, after passing Bossom's Boatyard, cross river by via a footbridge.

1.5   9.6   Continue along the river bank, keeping straight on when confronted by
(497076)   another path which comes from over the bridge on your left. Go over a further footbridge, onto a long narrow island. Eventually you will reach an inlet which gives access to the end of the Oxford Canal. Cross this by a footbridge. Keep following the main river as far as the next road bridge, where the path ends. Turn ← along the road. The walk ends at Oxford station (503063) which is some 300 yards away. You may enter the station either by going up the driveway on the left or you can
1.0   10.6   go under the railway bridge then turn left into the main entrance.

Check your platform. Trains for the Cotswold Line can leave from any of them. Trains for the Reading and London direction all depart from Platform 1. There are various refreshment outlets at Oxford station and public toilets are available on the station concourse or on platform 2.

There are so many things you could say about **Oxford** and we could not possibly do justice to the city by trying to give details of its multitude of attractions here. Suffice it to say that it one of the top tourist attractions in England. If you have an hour or two before your train, and if you have any energy left following your walk, you may continue straight on beyond the station for a half mile or so into the city centre and have a look around. Alternatively, two open-top bus services operate from the station forecourt and these take in many of the university colleges.

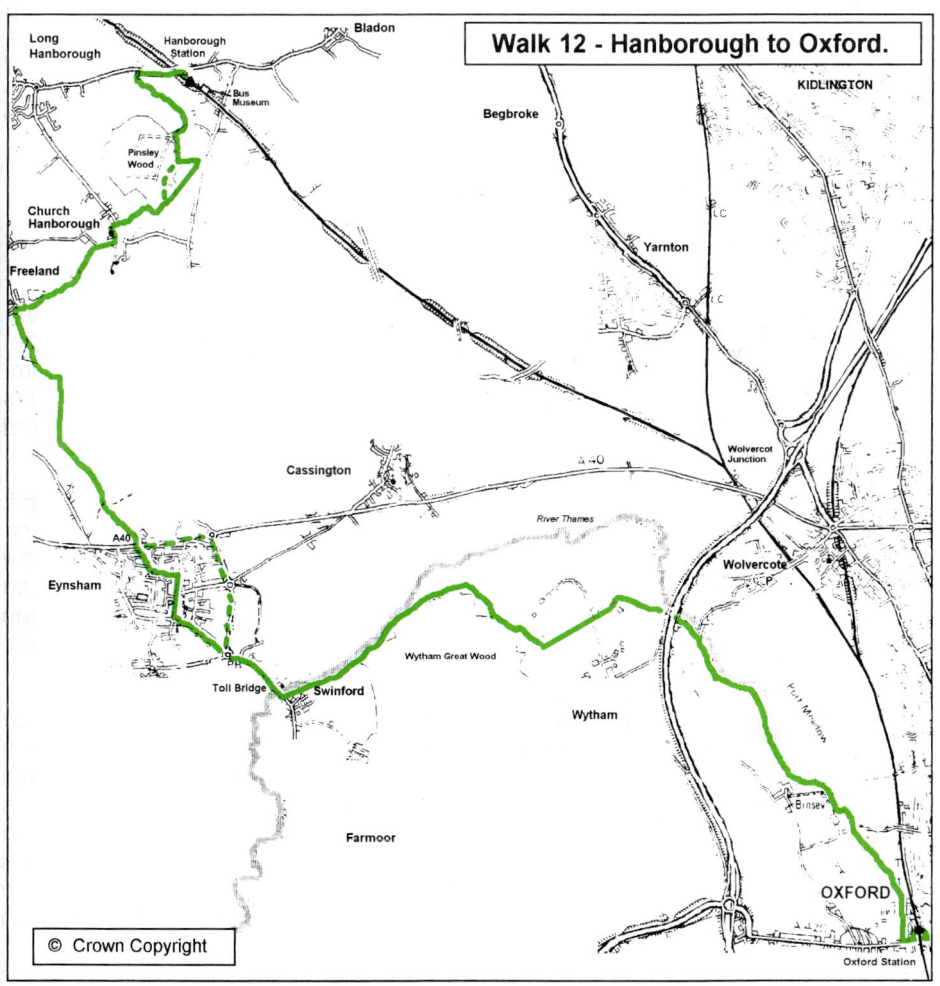

Walk 12 - Hanborough to Oxford.

© Crown Copyright

DIRECTORY of PLACES SERVED BY THE WALKS

Place Name	Walk No(s)	Information or Comments.
Ascott-under-Wychwood	10	RS, PH, S, ☎.
Aylton	1	BB.
Bledington	9	PH, BB, ✉ /FS, ☎.
Blockley	8	PH, FS, ✉, H, ☎.
Broad Campden	8	PH, BB, ☎.
Broadwell	9	PH, BB, ☎.
Callow End	4	PH, FS/✉.
Charlbury	10,11 & 11A	RS, PH, S, ✉, H, BB, YH, FS, PT, ☎.
Chilson	10 & 11A	☎
Chipping Campden	8	PH, FS, ✉, H, PT, BB, TI, ☎
Church Hanborough	12	PH, ☎.
Colwall	2 & 2A	PH, FS, H, ✉, ☎.
Combe	11	RS, (½ mile from station: PH, S/✉), ☎.
Cropthorne	6	PH, BB, ✉, ☎.
Drakes Broughton	5	PH, FS, ✉, ☎.
Donnington	9	☎.
East End	11	PH, BB.
Eastnor	2A	FS/✉.
Evesham	6 & 7	RS, PT, PH, S, CF, ✉, BB, TI, FS, ☎
Eynsham	12	PH, PT, S, CF, ✉. ☎
Finstock	11 & 11A	RS, PH, S/✉.☎
Fladbury	6	PH, FS, BB, ✉, ☎.
Hampton Bishop	1	PH.
Hawbridge	5	PH, ☎.
Hereford	1	RS, PH, H, PT, CF,✉ , BB, FS, TI, ☎.
Honeybourne	7 & 8	RS. FS/✉, ☎
Kempsey	5	PH, FS, S, ✉, ☎.
Kingham	9 & 10	RS, ☎. (In village, not on route: PH, H, S/✉).
Ledbury	1,2 & 2A	BR, PH, H, PT, S, CF, ✉, FS, TI, ☎
Longborough	9	PH, BB, S/ ✉, ☎.
Long Hanborough	11 & 12	RS. PH, S, ✉, BB. FS, ☎.
Littleworth	5	☎.
Lower Moor	6	FS, ✉, ☎.
Madresfield	4	☎
Malvern	2,2A & 3	RS(2), PH, H, PT, ✉, FS, TI, YH, ☎
Middle Littleton	7	☎.
Mordiford	1	PH, FS, BB, ✉.
Moreton-in-Marsh	8 & 9	RS, PH, H, PT, BB, S, FS, TI, ✉, ☎.
Oddington	9	PH, FS/ ✉, ☎.
Offenham	7	PH, FS, ✉, ☎.
Oxford	12	RS, S, PH, H, PT, CF, ✉, BB, TI, YH, ☎
Pershore	5 & 6	RS, S, PH, H, CF, ✉, BB, ☎
Powick	4	PH, S.
Putley Green	1	✉.
Shipton-under-Wychwood	10	RS, S, ✉, BB, PH, H, FS. ☎
Weston sub Edge	8	PH, FS/✉.
Woolhope	1	PH, BB, ✉